CARMARTHENSHIRE VILLAGES

CARMARTHENSHIRE VILLAGES

Geoffrey Davies

SIGMA Leisure

Published by Sigma Leisure - an imprint of
Sigma Press, Stobart House, Pontyclerc, Penybanc Road, Ammanford, Carmarthenshire SA18 3HP.

British Library Cataloguing in Publication Data
A CIP record for this book is available from the British Library.

ISBN: 978-1-85058-943-3

Typesetting and Design by: Sigma Press, Ammanford.

Cover photograph: Felingwm Uchaf © Geoffrey Davies

Drawings: © Geoffrey Davies

Printed by: TJ International Ltd, Padstow, Cornwall

Contents

Introduction

Carmarthenshire is one of the most beautiful counties in Britain, yet is often overlooked by the tourist racing towards the beaches of Pembrokeshire. It is essentially a rural county with the majority of the population living in villages and smaller communities. There is ample evidence of pre-Roman settlement in the county and many villages have their origins in the Dark Ages, before written documentation.

The aim of this book is to give a guide to the county's smaller communities, with a brief description, a little history and some stories of village characters. A sad aspect of researching for this book has been the witnessing of the rapid changes affecting village life. Rural pubs are disappearing as are village shops, post offices and schools. Much of the development in the more rural areas has been up-market, attracting older occupiers, often to the detriment of village life.

With the exception of Ammanford, Carmarthen and Llanelli, the towns of Carmarthenshire are little more than villages. Indeed, W. F. Deacon in his *Innkeeper's Album* of 1823 referred to the "village of Llandilo Vauhr, which the natives in their simplicity dignify by the name of a town". These towns do however have a long history and are the subject of books in their own right and outside the scope of this book. There are, on the other hand, villages larger in population than small towns, which have developed into suburbs, but they tend to retain a village community spirit, and are included.

Where possible an English translation of the Welsh name is included. Where the meaning is open to doubt, an explanation is offered in the text. Councils across Wales have installed signs translating English names into Welsh (not always accurately), but not the other way round, which would help the majority monoglot English speakers and visitors extend their Welsh vocabulary.

The exception to this is the numerous villages beginning 'Llan'. Llan is strictly the circular ground on which a church was built, but has become synonymous with church. The saint to which the church is dedicated is given in the text. Many Celtic saints date from the Dark

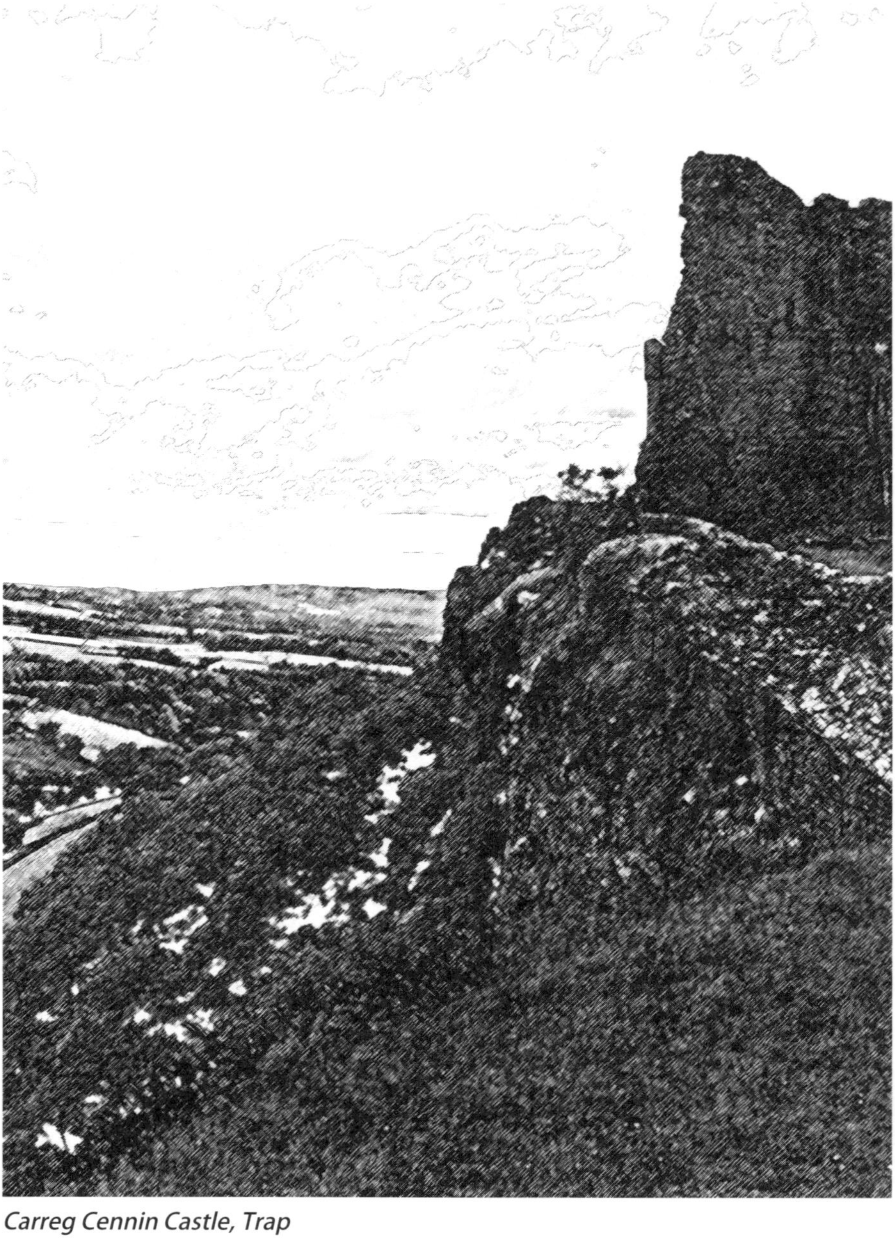

Carreg Cennin Castle, Trap

Ages and we are left with myths and legends to identify them. Brychan, King of Brycheiniog, had between 12 and 63 children, depending on which of the Welsh, Irish, Cornish or Breton versions you believe, but all his children seem to have been saints, including St Tybie of Llandybie.

The early history of the county was written in the 12th century, by writers who often had an interest in promoting certain ideas and interests. In an attempt to enhance the reputation of their cathedral and its income from pilgrims, monks at Llandaff, for example, claimed that St Teilo had been the second Bishop of Llandaff, though there is no evidence to support this. His body was claimed to be buried at Llandeilo, Llandaff and at Penally in Pembrokeshire where he was born. To explain this contradiction it was claimed that, on his death, the three churches laid claim to his body but, unable to agree, they prayed and, lo and behold, the next morning there were three bodies. Miracles were used to explain things which seemed impossible, for example the lake of Llyn Llech Owain at Gorslas or the impressions in the stone at Pumsaint.

With the Normans came written history but also the battles and castles. There was however intermarriage and the old Welsh families survived and eventually prospered, especially after Henry Tudor, who traced his ancestry back to the Lord Rhys of Deheubarth, became King Henry VII. Much of the wealth of the county was concentrated in the hands of a few families whose names crop up with regularity. Great pride was exhibited in ancestral research as this comment in the 1829 *Mirror* magazine illustrates: “a Welshman is almost proverbially distinguished for deeming himself illustriously descended and relating his long pedigree”. These families benefited not only from the land but from the mineral wealth and industry that followed in the south-east of the County.

Welsh is one of the oldest spoken languages in the world, but the rules for written Welsh are relatively recent. This led to place-names being spelt in an anglicized form. For example, the spelling of Llanelli was Llanelly and used as such in company names. Even anglicized names have changed their spelling. Laugharne, which is derived from the Welsh ‘Talacharn’, was spelt ‘Langharne’ by Mary Curtis in her 1871 book with a note to the effect that the use of the ‘u’ rather than ‘n’ was modern. When quoting from texts the original spelling has been used. (Talacharn was not the original Welsh name, Talycoran and Anercoram were the earlier terms, meaning Mouth or End of the Goram stream that flows into the Taf.)

Villages of Carmarthenshire

Aberarad (Mouth of the Arad)

The village, just south-east of Newcastle Emlyn, is an attractive mix of old and new housing with light industry near the junction of Station Road and Old Carmarthen Road. The Afon Arad has been piped underground.

Now a suburb of Newcastle Emlyn, where the Arad joins the Teifi, Aberarad was the site of the Newcastle Emlyn Union Workhouse, known as Foelallt Castle, completed in 1839. It was designed for 150 inmates but never reached capacity with the number of casual vagrants outnumbering inmates. In 1924 part of the workhouse was rented for cheese production by the West Wales Farmers Dairy Society and part was converted into flats for those awaiting housing locally. Today it is the site of a factory manufacturing Mozzarella cheese, which is sold worldwide. Some parts of the workhouse remain in the modern complex.

There were two mills in Aberarad, East Melyn and Pandy Woollen Mill, both on the Arad. The latter was owned by the King and all who lived within the area were forced to use its products. The pretty cottages of Mill Street, tucked away in the centre of the old village, mark the site of these mills.

Aber Bowlam (Mouth of the Bowlam)

Aber Bowlan is a tiny hamlet south-west of Caio. In 1876, Judge John Johnes of Dolaucothi was murdered at Caio by his butler, Henry Tremble, who subsequently shot himself. Tremble was buried at Caio at 11 o'clock at night, but the villagers were concerned that he was buried in the same churchyard as his victim and the body was exhumed and taken to Llandulas in Breconshire at night and buried there. The parishioners of Llandulas took exception to this and decided to return the body. They intended to arrive at Caio in the middle of the night, but lost their way arriving after dawn. Panicking, they dumped the coffin on the path leading to the churchyard with a note attached. At Aber Bowlam they threw out the straw which had been used to cover the coffin and there it remained for a number of years, a 'Bwgan' (a bogey) to frighten children.

Just off the crossroads are the remains of Capel Aber Bowlam, a Methodist chapel. The roof has gone and part of the north wall has collapsed, with scrub growth inside and outside the ruins.

Aber-Giar (Mouth of the Giar)

Aber-giar is, in effect, an extension of Llanllwni on the A485. It stands between the Nant Iar and Nant Ceiliog. There are no signs to mark the start and end of the hamlet, but the Belle Vue Inn marks the southern boundary. It is a ribbon development of mixed age, low density housing.

Abergorlech (Mouth of the Gorlech)

Abergorlech is a tranquil village in the beautiful tree lined Cothi valley where the River Gorlech meets the Cothi. The village grew from a single 16th century house, Ty Mawr. The bridge over the Cothi, with very irregular arches, dates from the same era and is one of the oldest surviving bridges in the county. When I visited the village, Ty Mawr was undergoing renovation. A previous owner was Henry Price, Lord Lieutenant of Carmarthen in 1649. In the 1830s the house was sold to a William Jones who converted it into the Wheatsheaf Inn, though there are no external signs today of its life as a tavern.

The church of St David dates from 1834 and was previously a chapel of ease, meaning that it was a place of worship open to different Christian sects, notably the Methodists who held regular services there in the 1740s. Daniel Rowland, one of the leading figures in Welsh non-conformity, and William Williams Pantycelyn, the poet and hymn writer, are known to have preached here. The interior of St David's is noted for the magnificent brass oil lamps.

Capel Newydd (New Chapel), opened in 1828, was the third Independent chapel serving the village though its predecessors were built on the other side of the river.

The Black Horse is a lively local inn offering food. It can be assumed there was a settlement here prior to the 16th century from the name of the poet Dafydd Gorlech, one of the Poets of the Nobility, who lived during the mid 15th century.

Abergwili (Mouth of the Gwili)

Abergwili lies on the banks of the River Towy just outside Carmarthen and at the foot of Merlin's Hill. Today the village is by-passed by the A40. The Carmarthen County Museum, once the Palace of the Bishops of St David's, houses a wide collection illustrating the history of the county. The building which has been in constant use since 1290, first as a college for priests and then as the Bishop's Palace, was largely rebuilt in 1903 following a fire, but parts of the older palace remain, including the chapel built by William Laud when he was Bishop of St David's. He went on to become Archbishop of Canterbury and was beheaded during the English Civil War. It was in this building that the New Testament was first translated into Welsh. The last remnant of Merlin's Oak is on display as are the friezes from the Picton Memorial, depicting the local hero of the Battle of Waterloo. The parish church of St David was rebuilt in 1841. Legend has it that the stone used for the top of the spire was from the post to which Bishop Ferrer of St David's was tied when he was burnt for heresy in Carmarthen under Mary Tudor in 1555.

In medieval times, Abergwili was a thriving town with 25 burgesses and a weekly market. The college for priests was moved in 1541 from Abergwili to Brecon on the grounds that "the people in the southern parts of Wales were rude and ignorant and unskilled in the English tongue". The college was then converted to the Bishop's Palace.

Above Abergwili stands Merlin's Hill. The site of a pre-Roman hill fort, legend has it that a cave on the hill was home and tomb to Merlin, magician to King Arthur, and that he was locked there in bonds of enchantment by his lover. There are trails up to the fort which offers views over Carmarthen and the Towy valley.

Abernant (Mouth of the Stream)

Abernant is a small scattered village five miles west-north-west of Carmarthen. The parish was once the site for Carmarthen Races. The picturesque church of St Lucia is reputed to have the largest graveyard in Wales. The village alternated with Bwlchnewydd as the venue for the leet court for the hundred, judging minor misdemeanours. An insight into life at the start of the 19th century can be gleaned from an entry in the parish records of a £5 fine being imposed on the family of Jane David for burying her in material other than wool. Half the fine was distributed among the poor of the parish and the remainder given to the informant.

James Howell was born at Abernant in 1594, where his father was the vicar, and at the age of sixteen went to Jesus College Oxford. In 1627 he was elected MP for Richmond in Yorkshire but in 1643 he was thrown into Fleet prison in London following the confiscation of his correspondence and manuscripts. While in prison he published *Epistolae Ho-Elianae* (*Familiar Letters*) and the profits from the third edition were used in the founding of Guy's Hospital. He was released after eight years and devoted himself to the interests of Cromwell; though he also found favour with Charles II and became Histographer Royal. He was a linguist, publishing works in Spanish, Portuguese and Welsh. Following his death in 1666, he was buried in Temple Church in London where there is a monument to him. His elder brother Thomas, born at Llangamarch, where their father was perpetual rector, became Bishop of Bristol.

Alltwalis

A hamlet on the A485, the name Alltwalis can be traced back to 1624 when it was Tire Allt Dwalais, though its origin is obscure. Some believe it refers to a local brigand, Walis, who lived in a cave locally, though the more likely meaning going back to the 1624 spelling is 'the wooded slope near the Dwalais brook'.

Troedyrhiw Independent Chapel was established in 1784, rebuilt in 1832 and again in 1897. On my visit it had a distinctly neglected appearance. There is an inn, the Masons Arms, on the hill towards the north end of Alltwalis.

The Alltwalis Wind Farm, consisting of ten turbines, was completed in 2009.

Babel

Babel is a small hamlet in the parish of Llanfair ar y Bryn north-east of Llandovery. Pantycelyn Farm, the home of William Williams Pantycelyn, writer of the original Welsh hymn *Bread of Heaven*, lies three quarters of a mile west of the telephone box. There is an information board at the farm entrance.

Bancffosfelen (Mill on the Dyke on a Hill)

Bancffosfelen is a village on the B4306 Pontyberem to Carmarthen road. There is largely ribbon development on the hill out of Pontyberem as the road rises to Mynydd Llangyndeyrn. The lower part is almost exclusively early 20th century development with newer houses higher up the hill. Pisgah Welsh Baptist chapel was established in 1872 and rebuilt in 1899 and stands on a side road opposite the school. The name suggests that there was once a mill on this hillside, but no trace can be found today.

Bancycapel (Chapel Bank)

Bancycapel is a small hamlet set in open farmland on a hill on the B4309 Pontyates to Carmarthen road. It is named after the small Calvinistic Methodist chapel on the hill. There has been a small amount of modern development.

Banc-y-felin (Mill Hill)

Bancyfelin is a village now by-passed by the A40. It has, in the 1990s, expanded with new housing along the main street and the Werndale Private Hospital. Two large farms either side of the village show its agricultural heritage, but the village now acts as a commuter base for nearby Carmarthen. At the centre of the village is the Fox and Hounds, a thriving local pub and restaurant. The name of the village denotes a mill on the hill, but no evidence of the mill remains.

For such a small village, it has produced a relatively large number of international rugby players, including Delme Thomas and Mike Phillips, but perhaps the most remarkable son of the village was James Ira Thomas 'Taffy' Jones DSO, MC, DFC & Bar, MM.

Starting as a radio mechanic in the Royal Flying Corps in World War I, Jones graduated to observer and was then commissioned and trained as a pilot. Despite a reputation for crash landings (28) Jones made 37 'kills' in a short 3 month piloting career. After the war he remained with the RAF, retiring in 1936. With the outbreak of World War II, he was recalled as Chief Signals Officer Training before going on to become Officer Commanding the Number 7 Bombing and Gunnery School at Porthcawl. While in this role, flying an unarmed Hawker Henley near Swansea, he attacked a Junkers JU 88 bomber with a flare gun, forcing the German plane to break off its attack. After the war Jones retired to Aberaeron, though he is buried at Cana Chapelyard, Bancyfelin.

Bancyffordd (Road on the Breast of a Hill)

Bancyffordd is a ribbon hamlet of mainly new bungalows south of Llandysul in the north of the county, along a road running down to the Teifi valley.

Bethlehem

Bethlehem is named after its chapel and is celebrated in the run up to Christmas by the special postmark on cards posted in the village. The village school is now the village hall and post office, but apart from its name there is little of interest in the village itself. Above the village, however, stand the twin hill forts of Garn Goch, the largest in Wales. The loose stone walls of Garn Goch Fawr are still impressive as is the cairn within. The fort offers views over the Towy valley as far as Merlin's Hill in the west and the hills above Llandovery to the north-east. The forts are Bronze Age in origin, pre-dating the Iron Age. At the time of the Roman invasion, the Dematae were the Celtic tribe occupying Wales west of the Towy while the Silures, a more warlike tribe, occupied lands to the east.

Below the fort is a memorial stone erected in 2006 to Gwynfor Evans, MP for Carmarthenshire, a leading Welsh language campaigner and the first Plaid Cymru Member of Parliament.

A little to the north of Bethlehem, on the Towy side of the road, there used to stand Dan yr Allt, a late Elizabethan mansion owned by the Lloyd family. Admiral William Lloyd (Admiral of the White) left the estate to his cousin Sir John Stepney who lived abroad and the mansion fell into decay and was demolished in 1841. On Stepney's death the house reverted to the Lloyd family and the Reverend Henry Robert Lloyd, curate of Llangadog in the 1830s, described the house as having been much altered with small rooms with Elizabethan fireplaces and a chapel decorated with blue and gold stars.

Betws

Betws today is barely distinguishable from Ammanford, just across the River Aman, but it is a much older village and at one time was much larger than the neighbouring town. The name Betws is Welsh for oratory, but it is thought to be a corruption of the Anglo Saxon 'bedehus', a form of almshouse where the poor were given shelter in return for praying for their benefactor. The church of St David was extensively renovated in 1872, but some 60% is still 14th century or earlier. The llan or churchyard would appear to have been much larger, with part having been cut off by Betws Road.

Until 1817, Betws was only accessible by mountain road from Swansea and Neath. Its sense of isolation can be gathered from the local phrase "Betws and the World".

In 1844 there was some quarrying for slate, and coal and iron mining, but the rural nature of the parish at that time meant the main production was of cheese and butter. This was to change at the end of the 19th century with the opening of the Ammanford No 1 mine, in 1890, and the Ammanford No 2, in 1891, closing in 1925 and 1976 respectively. Mining continued with the Betws drift mine opening in 1976 and was the last major mine to close in the county in 2003.

For a relatively small village Betws has produced a large number of famous sons, including the singer Donald Peers, Wales' first Secretary of State Jim Griffiths MP, whose father was the village blacksmith and his brother the poet Amanwy, and Ivor Richard, MP, later Baron Richard of Ammanford, a European Commissioner and Lord Privy Seal.

Today Betws is primarily a dormitory village for Ammanford with new housing. The last evidence of the coal industry is gradually disappearing and a wind farm is being developed on Betws Mountain. The Mountain offers extensive views as far as Pembrokeshire on a clear day. There are the scant remains of a castle – Castell Penlle'r – a dry stone building dating from the 13th century, which must have been a dreadful place to be stationed in the middle of a cold damp Welsh winter.

Blaenau (Tips)

Blaenau is a village between Llandybie and Cross Hands, running into Cae'r Bryn. A good mix of early 20th century and modern housing, together with a primary school and the Badgers inn, make for an attractive residential area. The area to the south of the village was an opencast mining site but has now been restored. The railway line from Cross Hands to Tirydail passed to the south of the village. It was a freight only line and closed in 1962 though with the track removed it was used by lorries in the open cast workings.

Blaenwaun (Front Moor)

A village on the St Clears to Tegryn road in the north of the county, it has a mixture of older and modern housing stretching along the main road and the side road to Cwmfelin Mynach. There is a local pub, the Lamb Inn, but no church or chapel in the village, but Moriah Independent Chapel, established in the 1820s and rebuilt in 1885, stands just north. At 220 metres Blaenwaun is one of the highest villages in south-west Wales. There is a wind farm to the west, while to the east are the sites of two hill forts: Castell Mawr and Castell Bach on either side of the wooded valley of the Afon Sien.

Blaenycoed (Front of the Woods)

A hamlet in the parish of Cynwyl Elfed situated north of Abernant and east of Cynwyl Elfed. The Independent Chapel was built in 1805. The chapel room next to the chapel was once the Blaen y Coed Inn. Further down the hill from the chapel, past the small terrace of houses, is the old smithy.

Brechfa (A Hilly Place)

Brechfa is a small village in the beautiful Cothi valley, though the name now is better known for the forest to the north. The village has been inhabited since the 6th century. A well on the banks of the River Morlais was used for baptism by Bishop Teilo and the church became St Teilo's. In the 13th century the church came under Talley Abbey and the monks established a grange or farmstead in the parish. On the Dissolution of the Monasteries under Henry VIII, the forest, then known as Glyncothi, passed to the Crown.

The present church dates from 1893, replacing the old church which was dilapidated and too small for the congregation. The appeal letter stated "The floor is made of mortar, and the ceiling flat like that of an ordinary room. There is not a single architectural feature in the whole building. It is in every respect unfit and unworthy of the holy purposes to which it has been dedicated." The new church was designed by E H Lingen-Barker whose designs can be seen in parish churches in England and Wales.

Opposite the church stands the Forest Arms Hotel (now closed), a former landlord of which owned a raven called Bob who, the story goes, would steal the caps of boys on their way to school, take eggs from the vicar's chickens and peck the rears of carters' horses causing them to gallop off while the carters were drinking at the bar.

Brechfa was, until the 1920s, a centre for the manufacture of charcoal and, more unusually, oil, with works beyond a field south-west of the church. In 1933 the writer Gareth Jones describes the process of getting oil from the charcoal production: "From the oven the vapours were led in pipes passing through a pond which acted as a water condenser. These vapours were condensed into tar, water-and oil, which were collected into 'sumps' (or receivers or tar-wells), as used in a modern gas-works. The tar went into one receiver and the oil into another. The watery oil was then pumped into vats and mixed with lime.

This mixture of oil and lime was then churned in the old-fashioned way, as if it were cream. It was churned until there was a froth on top. It was then allowed to settle down, and then put into a big boiler, where it was boiled. It then became vapour again and was carried out in vaporous form through a pipe into a cask in the naphtha room. After various other processes the residue was left in different barrels until the final light oil was produced."

The forest was developed for modern forestry in the 1930s as an employment scheme and today provides a combination of forestry and leisure activities with numerous forest walks and bike trails.

Broad Oak (Derwen Fawr)

Broad Oak is a hamlet just north of Llangathen and Aberglasney House and gardens on the A40.

It is believed to be the site of one of the two battles of Cadfan in 1257 between the Welsh and English. An army consisting of English, Gascon and Welsh troops under Stephen Bauzan, Lord of Breigan and Llansannor landed at Carmarthen on 12th May, 1257 and marched on Dinefwr Castle, Llandeilo. They intended to restore Rhys Fychan, grandson of the Lord Rhys and a supporter of Henry III, to lands stripped from him by Llewellyn of Gwynedd. The Welsh had hidden their forces in the woods and harried the English. Rhys while making an attempt to persuade the garrison at Dinefwr Castle to surrender was taken prisoner and changed sides. The English then decided to retreat to Carmarthen and were attacked at Coed Llathen, believed to be in the vicinity of Cadfan Farm, just to the north of Broad Oak, losing their supply train. Continuing their retreat towards Carmarthen, the English army were attacked at Cymerau, the area around the confluence of the rivers Cothi and Towy. The combination of woodland and marshy ground was impossible for the heavy English cavalry and between two and three thousand, including Stephen Bauzan lost their lives. Cadfan Farm is a Grade II Listed Building and has an upper banqueting hall dating from the 15th century.

Bronwydd (Wooded Hillside)

Originally known as Bronwydd Arms, after the inn established on land owned by the Bronwydd Estate of Henllan in Ceredigion, Bronwydd is a village in the beautiful, wooded Gwili valley, three miles north-west of Carmarthen at the junction of the B4301 and the A484. The Bronwydd Arms closed in 1978 and was demolished in 1981. A plaque opposite the main road junction marks the site. In 1841 there were just 15 properties in the village but with the coming of the railway, in 1860, and more recent development the population is near 600.

Bronwydd Arms station marks the start of the Gwili Steam Railway, part of the Carmarthen to Aberystwyth line, which closed in 1965. The Gwili Railway Company was formed in 1975 and by 1978 had acquired eight miles of track bed and started operating on one mile of track.

The church of St Celynin was built in 1894 at the edge of the village on the B4301. St Celynin is believed to have been from Ceredigion and lived in the 5th and early 6th centuries.

Today the village has a large number of new houses and serves as a commuter village for Carmarthen. Just outside the village on the road to Llanpumsaint is the Felinfach Horse Racing stables with its 42 acres of track, gallops, equestrian pool and other facilities.

Brynaman (Aman Hill)

Brynaman is a village partly in Carmarthenshire (Upper Brynaman) and partly in Neath Port Talbot (Lower Brynaman), high in the Aman Valley beneath the Black Mountain. Originally known as Y Gwter Fawr or the Big Gutter, the coming of the railways required a more respectable name and Brynamman was chosen. With the codification of the written Welsh language in the second half of the 19th century, the Welsh spelling was amended to Brynaman.

George Borrow in *Wild Wales* writes "As I descended I heard every now and then loud noises in the vale, probably proceeding from stone quarries. When I had proceeded about a mile I saw blazes down below, resembling those of furnaces, and soon after came to the foot of the hill. Crossing a bridge over a kind of torrent, I found myself amongst some houses. I entered one of them from which a blaze of light and a roar of voices proceeded, and, on inquiring of an old woman who confronted me in the passage, I found that I had reached my much needed haven of rest, the tavern of Gutter Vawr in the county of Glamorgan. At about eight o'clock on the following morning I got up and looked out of the window of my room, which fronted the north. A strange scene presented itself: a roaring brook was foaming along towards the west, just under the window. Immediately beyond it was a bank, not of green turf, grey rock, or brown mould, but of coal rubbish, coke and cinders; on the top of this bank was a fellow performing some dirty office or other, with a spade and barrow; beyond him, on the side of a hill, was a tramway, up which a horse was straining, drawing a load of something towards the north-west. Beyond the tramway was a grove of yellow-looking firs; beyond the grove a range of white houses with blue roofs, occupied, I suppose, by miners and their families; and beyond these I caught a sight of the mountain on the top of which I had been the night before – only a partial one, however, as large masses of mist were still hanging about it. The morning was moist and dripping, and nothing could look more cheerless and uncomfortable than the entire scene. Having been informed that there was a considerable iron foundry close by, I thought it would be worth my while to go and see it. I entered the premises, and was standing and looking round, when a man with the appearance of a respectable mechanic came up and offered to show me over the place. I gladly accepted his offer, and he showed me all about the iron foundry. I saw a large steam- engine at full play, terrible furnaces, and immense heaps of burning, crackling cinders, and a fiery stream of molten metal rolling along."

The inn which Borrow used was the Farmers Arms, later the Brynaman Hotel and now a private house and not to be confused with the New Farmers Arms which now forms part of the Rugby Club. The Farmers Arms was built in 1823 and the first railway, the Llanelly Dock Railway, arrived in 1846 to be followed some 18 years later by the Swansea Vale Railway. The railways were first used for freight, but in 1868 the first passengers arrived and the station was named Brynamman. Until then the only mention of Brynamman was

Brynamman House, built in 1838 and the first building in the village to have a slate roof.

The Gwter Fawr referred to the method of extracting coal in that a dam was built and water released to create a scouring action to reveal the coal just below the surface. No trace of the Gwter remains today. The road which leads over the Black Mountain from Brynaman was completed in 1819 and saw the beginnings of industrial development in the village. In the second half of the 19th century the village grew dramatically with a major expansion in mining and industry in Brynaman; a tin plate works was built in 1872 and the Ynys Colliery started in 1873. There was a consequent influx of workers with houses and chapels constructed to serve their needs.

Today Brynaman is a dormitory village with its pubs and access to the Black Mountain. But the public cinema is still operated as a trust and the open air lido was operated during the summer months until 2010 when it failed to open following damage in the previous winter. To the north of the village, a previous mining site has been transformed into a nature reserve: Ynys Dawela, with ponds and riverside and woodland walks.

St Catherine's Church was built in 1881. In World War II it suffered damage from a German bomb. On 10th July 1940 a German plane, pursued by British fighters, was separated after a raid on the English South coast. Flying over Brynaman, it targeted the rail marshalling yard but the bomb landed in the churchyard, causing severe damage to the church. In bearing the brunt of the blast, the church protected the nearby school.

Bwlchnewydd (New Pass)

Bwlchnewydd is a small rural village set in a wooded valley south of Cynwyl Elfed. To the south at Culcrug Farm was a hill fort and to the north a tumulus, indicating that the area has a long history of human habitation. A court leet for the hundred was held in the village, alternating with Abernant. This would be the equivalent of a magistrate's court, judging minor misdemeanours.

A little under two miles south of the village, on the Carmarthen road, stands the Plough and Harrow, where, in 1843, Rebecca rioters met before proceeding to Carmarthen. According to reports at the time there were some 4000 men on foot, led by Rebecca and 500 horsemen. They had been encouraged to leave their firearms behind but many carried cudgels and 'shallalaghs'. They marched through the town and were greeted by a crowd of onlookers. As well as country folk, there were reports of 'blackguards' from Carmarthen in their midst. They attacked the Union Workhouse but were put to flight by the Dragoons brandishing drawn swords.

The chapel at the northern end of the village was built in 1746, rebuilt in 1808, and enlarged in 1832. It is a Grade II Listed building. One of its ministers was Michael D Jones, raised in Bala, North Wales where his father was Principal of the Independent College. At the age of 26, Jones had travelled to the United States to study at first-hand the republican system and the institution of slavery. In 1848, he was ordained minister at Lawrence Street Chapel in Cincinnati and after two years returned to Wales as minister of Bwlchnewydd. In 1854 he took over from his father as Principal of Bangor Independent College. While in America he became concerned at the assimilation of Welsh speakers into the anglicized American language and became interested in the idea of establishing a Welsh speaking colony. In 1856 he called a meeting to further this idea and in 1862 joined forces with the Liverpool based Welsh Colonizing Society. He negotiated with the Argentine government and following an agreement that a self governing colony should be set up in Patagonia, the first 163 settlers left Liverpool on the Mimosa for Chubut in Patagonia. Though he did not travel with the settlers he largely financed the voyage. Known as the Father of the Colony, Jones only visited once in 1882, though his two sons joined the colonists. At home Michael D Jones was an advocate of a self-governing Wales within the United Kingdom.

Another minister at Bwlchnewydd was John Thomas, from 1842 to 1850. Thomas was a leading advocate of the abstinence movement and co-wrote the *History of the Independent Churches of Wales* with Thomas Rees, as well as other books. He went on to become chairman of the Union of Welsh Independents in 1878, and of the Congregational Union of England and Wales. He edited a number of periodicals connected with the Independent Churches.

Bynea

Once a major steel producing village, Bynea is now a suburb of Llanelli with a slightly run down appearance along Cwmfelin Road, despite new housing. Station Road and other developments to the north raise the character of the village. It has a railway station on the Heart of Wales Line and a thriving rugby club.

The derivation of the name is unclear. In Welsh it is 'Y Bynie', and one suggestion is that it is a corruption of 'heb un iau', meaning 'without a yoke', alluding to the practise of allowing oxen untethered in the river Loughor.

Cae'r Bryn (Hill Fort)

Cae'r Bryn is a former mining village on the road from Llandybie to Cross Hands. Today it has a mix of housing and a modern church, Eglwys Sant Marc. Outside the village hall is an old coalmine truck.

Caerbryn Anthracite Colliery was positioned on a rail track between Tirydail in Ammanford and Cross Hands. It opened in the 1850s and eventually three slant mines were in operation. At its peak it employed over 300 men. After 1900 production declined and Caerbryn had closed by the 1930s.

Caio

Caio or to give it its parish name Cynwyl Caio (Advanced Guards of Caius), today is a small attractive village north of the Llanwrda to Lampeter road. The village is dominated by its church with its battlemented tower, but some believe that it was a town of Roman origin known as the 'Red Town of South Wales'. Large amounts of red Roman brick have emerged from the plough and the village is close to the Roman gold mines at Dolaucothi. The name Caio is thought to derive from a Roman named Caius. Geraldus Cambrensis refers to it as 'Gaoi' in 1188.

There has been a church on the site since the 4th century, believed to have originally been constructed of wood. The present church, dedicated to St Cynwyl, is in the early English style and dates from the 13th century. A 6th century early Christian stone is built into the walls of the church. The lych-gate is particularly large with a window above the arch.

The church came under the control of Talley Abbey around 1200. The old Roman road Sarn Helen became a major drovers' route in the 18th century and Caio was the first stop on the route for Cardiganshire droves, with the blacksmith shoeing the cattle for their journey. Accommodation for drovers and animals was provided at

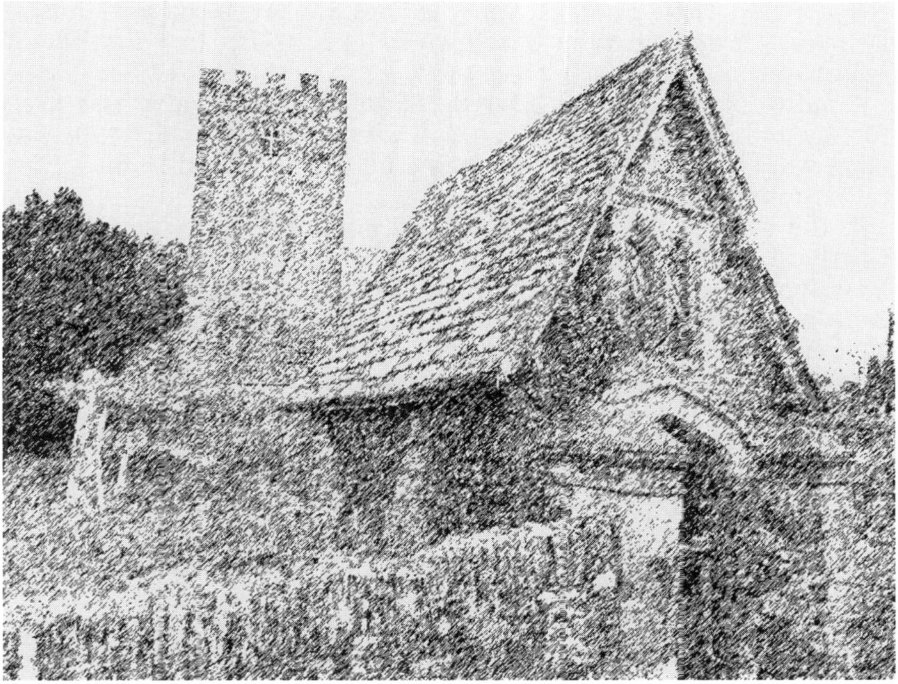

St Cynwyl church, Caio

Llundain Fechan Farm (Little London Farm). Drovers' enclosures survive as earthworks to the south of the village.

The inn, the Brunant Arms, is directly opposite the church and is named after local landowners, the Lloyds of Brunant. Brunant Mansion is situated on the road running from the Dolaucothi Gold Mine to Cwrt y Cadno. Known originally as Briw-nant or broken brook, the original house was late 16th century but rebuilt in the 18th century. The Brunant estate was once quite extensive, but has been split over the years through inheritance.

Caio was the stronghold of Gruffydd Ap Rhys, Prince of Deheubarth, following his return from exile in Ireland following the defeat and death of his father Rhys Ap Tewdor at the Battle of Brecon in 1093. This was where he brought the Princess Gwenllian following their marriage and it was from Caio that he launched raids on the Normans. Gruffydd and Gwenllian were killed in 1136 and 1137 respectively. Their youngest son, the Lord Rhys restored the lands of Deheubarth and, making peace with Henry II, became Justicar of South Wales.

A native of Caio, Morgan Dafydd Llewelyn of Rhydodyn was tried for the murder of the Chief Justice of Carmarthen who, in 1390, was slain while sitting in court. He came before Sir David Hanmer, the father-in-law of Owain Glyndwr

In the early 15th century, the local landowner was Llewelyn Ap Gruffydd Fychan whose sons fought alongside Owain Glyndwr. Llewelyn was captured by King Henry IV and, refusing to assist in the capture of Glyndwr, was publicly disembowelled and dismembered alive before the gates of Llandovery Castle. He is commemorated by a striking stainless steel statue erected alongside the castle in Llandovery.

The poet, outlaw and soldier, Lewis Glyn Cothi (died 1486) lived at Pwlltinbyd Farm. He served as an officer under Jasper Tudor, Earl of Pembroke and uncle of Henry Tudor who became Henry VII. A supporter of the Lancastrians during the Wars of The Roses, he lived for a while in Chester but was forced to leave before being arrested. There are some 230 of his poems preserved.

Buried in the churchyard at St Cynwyl's is Doctor John Harries, known as the 'Wizard of Cwrt y Cadno'.

In 1834 the Reverend Dr William Davies was engaged to teach the children of David Davies of Froodvale, a mansion on the west bank of the Cothi, south of Pumsaint. The Reverend Doctor took the opportunity to establish a school which became known as the Froodvale Academy. He built a small building on his own land on a hillside near the Llansawel to Pumsaint bridle path and filled it with desks and benches arranged "like pews in a church" with an aisle down one side. Within a short space of time the Academy had gained a high reputation and had up to 34 students, paying 15 shillings a quarter. This was a school for the sons of the local gentry preparing for higher education, many entering holy orders. The Academy closed in the 1850s.

In the 19th century this peaceful village was the scene of a notorious murder. The well respected Judge John Johnes of Dolaucothi was murdered by his sacked butler, Henry Tremble, an Irishman said to have had a fiery temper, in a dispute over the running of the village inn. After the murder Tremble committed suicide. Judge Johnes is buried in the churchyard, as is Tremble, though not before some controversy. It was ordered that Tremble should be buried at night, but the locals were concerned at a murderer being buried in the same cemetery as his victim, so the body was exhumed and transported at night to Llandulas graveyard in Brecknockshire and buried. On hearing this, the residents of Llandulas objected to having a murderer buried in their parish and exhumed the body and at night transported the coffin back to Caio. Unfortunately they got lost and arrived at Caio in daylight, panicked and fled the village leaving the coffin outside the church gate.

Judge Johnes' son in law, Lieutenant General Sir James Hills-Johnes VC GCB, known as the Hero of Delhi, retired to the parish and became High Sheriff of Carmarthenshire. He is also buried at Caio.

Perhaps Caio's most famous son was Roger Williams (1606-1683), son of William Williams of Maestroiddyn-Fawr Farm. He came to the attention of Sir Edward Coke, Chief Justice of the King's Bench, who sent him to Sutton Hospital School (now Charter House) from where he went to Jesus College Cambridge. (The principals of Jesus College from 1602-1620 had both come from the neighbouring parish of Llansawel).

Ordained as a minister in the Church of England, Williams became unsettled by the lack of religious freedom under Archbishop Laud and left for America. He arrived in Boston in 1631 and served as minister in the church but was banished in 1636, following his assertion: "That the Civil Power has no jurisdiction over the conscience". He fled to Rhode Island, setting up the settlement which became the town of Providence. He became President of the Colony of Providence in 1654 and is regarded as the founder of Rhode Island. A number of his descendants visited Caio in 1851 to see Williams' birthplace.

Capel Bwlchyrhiw (Chapel on the Hill Pass)

Capel Bwlchyrhiw, is situated on the pass between Cilycwm and Cwrt y Cadno with the Nant Melyn flowing east towards the Gwenffrwd and Towy and the Cothi flowing south-west towards Cwrt y Cadno. To find a chapel in such a remote spot can probably be attributed to the clamp-down on non-conformity after the Restoration of the Monarchy in 1660 and the 1665 Five Mile Act, which prohibited ministers preaching within five miles of their former church. This was one of the earliest Baptist congregations, meeting in this remote area as early as 1662. The earliest services were held in a cave, with the first chapel being built in 1717. The chapel was rebuilt in 1906 and renovated as recently as 2002. This is a remote but beautiful spot with the little white washed chapel set against the northern slopes of Mynydd Mallaen. At the highest point of the mountain are the Crugiau Merched or Ladies' Cairns as well as a number of standing stones. To the north Pen-y-raglan-wynt has a stone circle, cairn and tumulus, showing that this upland area has a long history of habitation, especially in the Bronze Age when Britain had a warmer climate.

Capel Dewi

A small village on the B4300, between Llandeilo and Carmarthen, in the parish of Llanarthney. The village takes its name from a chapel of ease dedicated to St David, which appears to have been taken over by Calvinistic Methodists. The village used to have two pubs and a non-conformist chapel, all of which are now closed. One of the best restaurants in Wales, Y Polyn, is just over a mile from the village.

The village gardens have a mosaic created by the Young Farmers with the guidance of local sculptor Simon Hedger, who was responsible for the sculpture of St David which stands in the Gardens.

Capel Hendre

Capel Hendre is the site of, and named after, a Calvinistic Methodist chapel established in 1775 but rebuilt and extended over the years. The village has expanded in recent years with large numbers of new houses. It is also the site of a major industrial estate providing work in the Ammanford area.

Capel Isaac

Capel Isaac is a hamlet in attractive farming countryside three miles north of Llangathen. It is named after and largely centred on the Independent Chapel of the same name, founded in 1672 but rebuilt in 1790 and again in 1846. The school opposite the chapel is now a private house. Maesteilo Mansion on the outskirts of Capel Isaac was built in the early 19th century. It was the home of Sir William Mansel, 10th Baronet who moved to Maesteilo after he sold Iscoed in Ferryside to Sir Thomas Picton. The mansion was converted to a hotel in 1979, but is now a care home. Nearby is St John's Church Maesteilo, a 19th century church, part of the Llandeilo ministry.

Capel Iwan

A small village in the north-west of the county taking its name from the Independent Chapel established here early in the 18th century. The chapel has been rebuilt and expanded. The village was agricultural but has expanded with new houses and bungalows. Capel Iwan hit the national headlines in 2010 when the school which had lost all its 12 pupils remained open for a year.

Capel Seion

The village is situated north-east of Pontyberem on the hills above the Gwendraeth Fawr. There are two chapel-like buildings on the site, the smaller of which is a hall built in 1907. The first Independent chapel was built in 1712, but worship had started here some time before. The chapel and hall have been rebuilt and renovated a number of times over the years.

A pleasant village, of mainly modern housing surrounded by farmland, has developed around the chapel.

Carmel

Carmel is best known today for its television transmitter mast, situated some way from the actual village, between Llandeilo and Cross Hands. Named after its chapel, the village is primarily a ribbon development.The small parish church of St Mary's is modern.

Carway / Carwe

Carway is a small former mining village on the River Morlais in the Gwendraeth Valley that has become the centre for major leisure activities.

Mining started nearby in the 1760s. Kymer was a mine owner from Pembrokeshire who owned mines at Pwll y Llygod and Great Forest, near Carway. He initially used the Gwendraeth Fawr for transportation, but it was narrow and only navigable at high tide and subject to shifts in channel direction into the estuary. In 1760, Parliamentary approval was sought, at Kymer's own expense, to construct a canal. The Act of Parliament was granted on 19 February, 1766; the first canal to be constructed in Wales. It opened in 1769 and closed in 1867. The canal ran from a place called Ythyn Frenig on the south bank of the Gwendraeth Fach, below Kidwelly, and terminated at Pwll y Llygod on the Gwendraeth Fawr. The canal, which had no locks, proved a great success and enabled a considerable trade to develop between Kidwelly and Ireland and the West Country. The canal eventually became the basis for the railway, though evidence of the cut to the Gwendraeth Fawr can still be seen at Pwll y Llygod. Kymer died in 1784 and his business was carried on by his four sisters who are attributed with the establishment of Carway as a village to house miners. The railway bridge near Carway is the oldest in Wales and the second oldest in the world.

A drift mine was established here in 1863 and anthracite continued to be mined until 1960. In 1945, there were 237 men employed at the Carway mine. On closure, miners were transferred to Cynheidre. After the closure of the mine, Carway became a centre for opencast mining, with sites to the north and south of the village. The southern site was at one time the largest opencast mine in Europe. With the ending of coal extraction, the land was restored and the northern site is now occupied by Glyn Abbey Golf Club and the southern by Ffos Las Racecourse.

The Glyn Abbey golf course was developed by British Coal and opened in 1992. Named after a local mansion, Glyn Abbey, this was the home, over the centuries, to a number of prominent Carmarthenshire families, including the Gwyn family. There was never an abbey here even though one of the buildings is named Chapel House. Until the 1640s it was referred to as Glyn Mansion, but suddenly acquired the Abbey title. In 1903 it was the temporary home of some Benedictine monks who had been expelled from France. They spent six months at Glyn Abbey before moving on to Cardigan. Today Glyn Abbey is home to a 'New Age' community.

Ffos Las is set in a natural amphitheatre and opened for racing in 2009 to great acclaim. It stages both flat and jump races and has the advantage of having been developed by a civil engineering company whose head, David Walters, was a keen racehorse owner. The course was officially opened on 28th August, 2009 by Sir Peter O'Sullivan. Future plans include a hotel and leisure complex.

Carway has seen new housing, especially on the northern side of the main road. Siloh Baptist Chapel, established in 1891 and rebuilt in 1906, was the only place of worship in Carway and appeared derelict on my visit.

Cefnbrynbrain (Back of Crow Hill)

Cefn Bryn Brain is a village on the southern side of the Black Mountain on the A4068 between Brynaman and Ystalyfera. The name means Back of Crow Hill, and Bryn Brain is just to the east. It was John Jones, the owner of Bryn Brain Farm and a small mine at Blaen Gurwen, who, in 1819, supervised the building of the road from Brynaman to Llangadog; he also built the road from Cwmllynfell to Brynaman.

The rail line between Brynaman and Swansea passed to the south of the village. It was opened in 1864 and continued in operation until 1950.

There was no coal mining in Cefn Bryn Brain, but residents would have worked in the colliery at nearby Cwmllynfell across the county line or travelled by train to one of the many pits in the area. The mountain above the village is littered with disused limestone quarries and shake holes, where an underground stream has created a cavern into which the surface has fallen, as well as a number of Bronze Age Cairns. Across the road from the village there is a large opencast mining operation.

Cefneithin (Furze Ridge)

Cefneithin is a former mining village near Cross Hands.

The Blaenhirwaun Colliery sank two shafts in the late 19th century, one of which was over 660 feet deep. Six major seams were mined, employing up to 585 men. In September 1955 an explosion killed five and injured thirteen miners. The mine closed in 1962 and the workforce was transferred to the Cynheidre pit. Coal was transported to Llanelli on the Mynydd Mawr Railway which ran through the village.

Tabernacl Independent Chapel was built in 1877.

Today the village shows little sign of its mining past. There is a fair amount of new housing and the village seems more open than many former mining villages.

Among its more famous sons are Welsh rugby legends Carwyn James and Barry John.

Cenarth

Gerald of Wales visited Cenarth in 1188 and wrote: "The noble river Teivi flows here, and abounds with the finest salmon, more than any other river of Wales; it has a productive fishery, which is situated on

the summit of a rock, at a place called Canarch Mawr*, the ancient residence of St Ludoc, where the river, falling from a great height, forms a cataract, which the salmon ascend, by leaping from the bottom to the top of a rock.... The church dedicated to St Ludoc, the mill, bridge, salmon leap, an orchard with a delightful garden, all stand together on a small plot of ground."
The Itinerary Through Wales and The Description of Wales by Geraldus Cambrensis (1188)

(*now known by the name of Kenarth, which may be derived from Cefn y Garth – the back of the wear, a ridge of land behind the wear.)

Cenarth strides the River Teifi, with half the village in Carmarthenshire and half in Ceredigion. It is one of the most picturesque villages in the county. I remember visiting Cenarth in the 1960s when coracle fishermen were active on the river below the falls. In the summer there are still the occasional sightings of the coracle and the visitor may be lucky enough to get a ride. August Bank Holiday sees coracle racing below the falls. Cenarth is home to the National Coracle Centre but its principal attraction remains the river with its falls and 18th century bridge. Built in 1788 by architect David Edwards, son of William Edwards the designer of the old bridge at Pontypridd. It carries a single carriage road but is still strong enough to carry the heaviest loads. Note the circular holes in the bridge designed to ease the load on the main arches, a feature developed for the bridge at Pontypridd, for many years the world's longest single arch bridge. They also provide added relief when the river is in flood.

The river emerges from a steep wooded valley to rush over the falls where salmon and sewin can be seen leaping in the autumn. On the Carmarthen bank is an old flour mill that now houses the Coracle Centre.

Below the bridge the valley broadens and on the Carmarthenshire bank is Ffynnon Llawddog (St Llawddfog's Well). One of the ancient holy wells of Wales, it now has a modern cover. St Llawddog (St Ludoc) lived in the 7th century. A son of the King of Usk, he was, according to tradition, responsible for many miracles. He is chiefly associated with North Wales where he was Abbot of Bardsey. There are a number of churches dedicated to him in Carmarthenshire and Pembrokeshire including Cenarth and Cilgerran. The parish church was rebuilt in 1872, but the font is 12th century or earlier. There was a Celtic monastic community here, of which the mill would have been part, as would the Old Brewhouse, now a coffee shop next to the Three Horseshoes.

Tourism means that the village is well served with two pubs, a coffee shop and teashop.

Cilycwm – full name Llanfihangel-yng-Nghilycwm (St Michael's in the Secluded Vale)

Cilycwm is an attractive village the origins of which are lost in time. Situated in the Towy valley above Llandovery away from the river, one theory was that the village was relocated as a result of the Plague, but the church predates the 1367 pandemic.

Cilycwm is an ancient village. At the time of the Norman invasion Cadifor was Lord of Caio and Cilycwm. Cadifor was a son of Selyf, a descendant of Rhodri Mawr, the first prince to rule the majority of Wales.

There is no written evidence of a church prior to 1340. An early church would have been a wooden structure and it is likely to have been dedicated to a Celtic saint. When the Normans arrived they built churches in stone and often changed the dedication with St Michael being a popular choice.

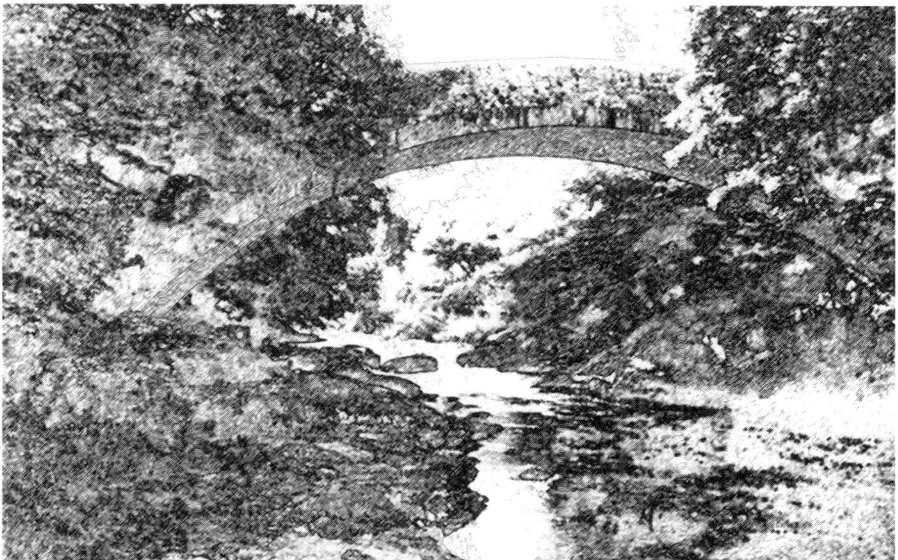

Dolauhirion Bridge, Cilycwm

The Grade I listed church of St Michael is particularly interesting with its twin aisles and wall paintings. It is listed as one of Sir John Betjeman's finest British churches. The original part of the church is the north aisle with its barrel vaulted roof dating from the early 1300s, while the south aisle dates from the 15th century and has a wagon roof. The wall paintings date from the 18th century; so it is somewhat confusing that the paintings, especially in the south aisle, seem to have been partly concealed by the timberwork. The Coat of Arms is unusual in that while similar to that used by George I, II and III between 1714 and 1801, the shield in the centre of the bottom left quarter depicts the Prince of Wales Feathers rather than the Imperial Crown of the Holy Roman Empire. Was this deliberate or a mistake by the original artist or the 'restorers'? The animals in the bottom left quarter represent the King's domains in Hanover. Note also the almost cartoon-like Irish Harp. There is also a skeleton depicting death on the west wall and a painted crucifixion above the altar.

Records show that the Rector of Cilycwm, Master John Hiot was released from parish duty in 1399 to serve Thomas Percy, Earl of Worcester. Thomas was the younger brother of Henry Percy, Earl of Northumberland. They challenged Henry IV at the Battle of Shrewsbury in 1403 but were defeated and Thomas Percy was hanged in public. What became of Master Hiot is not recorded

In the 18th and early 19th centuries, Cilycwm was a stop on the drove route from Caio. At that time there were no less than nine hostelries in the village.

For a small village Cilycwm has a large number of listed buildings including the vicarage, mill, post office, school, chapels and cottages.

Between Cilycwm and Llandovery the river is crossed by the New Bridge and further downstream by Dolauhirion Bridge. The Towy posed a problem for bridge builders at Llandovery and a wooden bridge had existed at Dolauhirion just north of the town since the 14th century. A stone bridge was built at Dolauhirion in 1773, to a design by William Edwards, by his son Thomas. It is now the oldest surviving bridge over the river and is classed as a Grade I listed structure. It was described by *The Field* magazine as the "prettiest bridge in all Britain" and a South American magazine named it in its list of the world's twelve most beautiful bridges. Typical of Edward's designs, it has circular holes either side of the main arch to provide added strength and provide additional relief in times of flood.

An Agricultural Society, an early trade union, was formed at a meeting in the Masons Arms, Cilycwm in July 1832, the same year the Tolpuddle Martyrs founded their Society. The difference was that the Cilycwm society did not swear oaths which was illegal under a 1797 Act.

The one remaining hostelry in the village is the Neuadd Arms, taking its name from Neuadd Fawr, which was once an impressive neo-classical mansion built in 1831. To the north of the village, it is now sadly in ruins. Neuadd Fawr was first mentioned in 1603 but the estate was enlarged in the early 19th century under the Davys family.

Another major property in the area is Henllys, to the south of the village. This 16th century property was bought for a Captain Williams by his father. Captain Williams, it appears, made a lot of money in India and used it to embellish Henllys, which is still a working farm estate with a bed and breakfast barn conversion.

Morgan Rhys (1716-1779) of Cilycwm, the son of Rhys and Anne Lewis, was a circulating teacher in the Welsh language, part of Griffith Jones of Llanddowror's team. Described as being a man of deep spirituality his salary as a teacher was just £4 a year. He wrote some of the finest hymns in the Welsh language including *O agor fy llygaid I weled*. He ranks alongside William Williams Pantycelyn in the history of Welsh hymn writing. He eventually settled in Llanfynydd where he died.

Cilymaenllwyd (Grey Stone Retreat)

Cilymaenllwyd is a parish in west Carmarthenshire taking in Efailwen, Glandy Cross and Login. There was no village and the parish church of St Philip and St James, which was situated near Login, is now a private dwelling. The name derives from the number of stone circles and cromlechs in the parish.

Court Henry

Court Henry takes its name from the house built by Henry ap Gwilym in the second half of the 15th century. Henry was a colourful character, having served in the army of Gascony. It is said that he fought and lost eight duels with Sir Thomas ap Griffith of Dinefwr. The house was renovated in the 19th century. The church of St Mary was built in 1832 for the family by the Reverend George Wade Green. The church was later enlarged in 1890 and again in 1892. The village lies to the north of the A40 and the village post office and community shop indicate that the village forms part of Dryslwyn.

Croesyceiliog (Cock Cross)

Croesyceiliog is an attractive, expanding village south of Carmarthen built across the valley of the Nant Cwm Croes-y-Ceiliog. The River Towy lies just 660 yards away to the west. Croesyceiliog Farm is at the centre of the village, but there is no place of worship. There are some older cottages near the farm but the majority of housing is modern.

Cross Hands

Cross Hands is now a sizeable shopping and industrial centre, either side of the A48 dual carriageway, but the older village to the south of the A48 contains a real Art Deco gem in the 1920 Public Hall. Still in use as a theatre, concert venue and cinema the hall is a Grade II listed building in Carmarthen Road.

There is a slightly run down feel to parts of the village as commerce has moved north of the old village. One theory for the village name is that it was an exchange point for prisoners between Swansea and Carmarthen jails. It was, however, the site of the Cross Hands Inn, a common name for inns on cross roads and it is almost certain that this is the true origin of the name.

The village grew in the 19th and early 20th centuries as a mining village, with Norton & Co opening the Cross Hands Colliery in 1869. At its peak in 1923, 859 were employed producing high quality anthracite from seven seams. Employment in the mines had dropped to 378 by 1960 and the collieries closed in 1962.

Crugybar (Cairn of the Peak or Heap of Wrath)

The name derives from the belief that the Romans buried their dead here after a defeat at the hands of the Britons under Buddug.

Crugybar is a scattered hamlet around the Bridgend Inn on the Lampeter to Llanwrda Road extending south towards Talley. The old school is now a community hall. There are no prehistoric features marked, but there is an unusual avenue on the ridge to the west of the community hall. Crugybar has given its name to a Welsh hymn tune which was used by Vaughan Williams in his *Three Preludes on Welsh Hymn Tunes.*

Crugybar is home to a leading Welsh Cob stud farm.

Felin Newydd (New Mill) is just opposite the Bridgend Inn. It is a 200 year old working watermill. It is thought that the site was previously occupied by a Roman mill. It was restored in the 1980s.

Crwbin (Hillock)

An attractive village on the B4306 as it descends from Mynydd Llangyndeyrn, with views over the valley of the Gwendraeth Fach and the village of Llangyndeyrn. A mixture of new and older houses, the village has an inn, the Three Compasses, and Ebenezer Independent Chapel which was established in 1829 and rebuilt in 1892.

Crwbin is known for its Silver Band, established in 1891, which won its section at the National Eisteddfod in 2009.

Mynydd Llangyndeyrn above Crwbin is rich in Neolithic and Bronze Age monuments. Among these are the Neolithic chambered cairns of Bwrdd Arthur and Gwal Y Ffiliast and a Bronze Age 10 foot standing stone known as Castell Twby, dated to 1090 BC, together with ring cairns and cist burials.

To the south-west of Crwbin are the remains of Capel Dyddgen. This church thrived in the 15th century when the tower was added. Some seven woollen mills were concentrated on the nearby Drysgeirch stream and it is thought that the little church would have served the religious needs of the workers. The church was in ruins when Fenton visited in 1809 and the remains of the tower are now ivy clad. At nearby Felindre, the mill still stands next to the stream.

Cwmann (Ann Valley)

Cwmann, the Ann Valley, is a village on the A 482 dropping down to the River Teifi which forms the Ceredigion border.

The Ram Inn, once voted Best Pub in Wales and fourth best in Britain, was the scene of a major drug handover in 1976, monitored by police as part of Operation Julie. One of the largest LSD production gangs in the world was operating in mid Wales and accounted for some 90% of the supply of LSD in Britain. Some 6 million 'tabs' of LSD worth £100 million were seized and 120 arrests were made in Britain and France. A listed building, the Ram closed in the early 2000s although plans were submitted for a new kitchen and restaurant in 2006.

The Cwmanne Tavern is situated at the bottom of the village. A 16th century inn once popular with drovers.

Cwm Du (Black Vale)

Cwm Du in the hills north of Llandeilo is a beautiful, tiny village on the Afon Dulais. The row of terraced cottages which houses the Cwmdu Inn, Post Office and shop is owned by the National Trust. The trust also owns Providence Baptist Chapel. Opposite the tavern is a mounting step from the time when horse riding was the common form of transport.

In 2009 the village received a visit from the Prince of Wales who enjoyed a pint in the Cwmdu Inn. The village community built a bridge behind the tavern to facilitate entry to the cricket field from the pub car park.

Just outside the village is a community known locally as Tipi village. Established in the 1970s on 200 acres, the village is a collection of Tipis, Yurts and round houses. The aims are ecological but essentially this is a 1970s hippy concept that has stood the test of time.

Cwmduad (Duad Vale)

Cwmduad is a village set in the wooded valley of the Afon Duad on the A484 Carmarthen to Newcastle Emlyn road. The little white washed church of St Alban sits on a small plot at the southern end of the village. In the centre of the village is a well preserved example of a Toll House. The village has retained its inn, the Afon Duad, which is at the northern end.

A little under a mile north of the village on a hill above the farm to the west of the road is Cerrig Llwdion, the remains of a substantial cromlech. Also to the west of the road and clearly visible from the road is Clawdd Mawr, a defensive earthwork of unknown date stretching for over a mile.

Cwmdwyfran and Pentre Morgan (Dwyfran Vale and Morgan Village)

Cwmdwyfran is a hamlet on the A484 in the Community of Bronwydd. It is on a bend of the River Gwili and was, in the 18th century, an area rich in oak woodland.

It is strange that this quiet spot was once the centre of an iron industry. The works were started in 1717 and taken over by Robert Morgan, in 1750, and continued under his son John and grandson Henry. In 1750, 120 tons of bar iron were produced at the forge, which was sited near Forge Farm and had a mill race connected to the river. Originally a corn mill, Cribyn Coch Mill stood on the site. It was the existence of the oak for charcoal and water for power that made Cwmdwyfran suitable for iron production. Iron ore and limestone were carried from the port of Carmarthen by mules and the resulting iron bars were sent to Carmarthen in the same way. Later, in the 18th century, coal was also brought to the works to be converted into coke and mixed with the charcoal to provide greater heat. The forge continued until 1830. Eventually the mill reverted to its original use for grinding corn.

In the 1790s John Morgan established the Carmarthen Furnace Bank, issuing its own notes and coins and an engraving of the Cwmdwyfran Iron Works was used on the coins.

The old blacksmith's forge continued until the late 1940s and the building is on the main road opposite the chapel.

The chapel was built in 1798 and rebuilt in 1909.

Pentre Morgan grew with the iron industry and once had a pub called the Morgan Arms. Today there is a pre-mixed concrete plant.

Cwmffrwd (Stream Vale)

Cwmffrwd is a 19th century village strung out along the A484 south of Carmarthen with further modern development. St Anne's Church is contemporary and is not a listed building.

The village lies on the route of a Roman road that led from Pensarn to Kidwelly.

360 yards north-east of Abercyfor Uchaf Farm are the earthworks of an Iron Age defended enclosure.

Cwmhiraeth (Vale of Yearning)

Cwmhiraeth is a village set in the lovely valley of the River Bran south-west of Drefach Felindre. A former mill village, there is a good mix of housing along the narrow, peaceful road running through the village.

Cwmifor (Ifor's Valley)

Cwmifor is essentially a village of modern houses off the A40 north-east of Llandeilo with the Victorian St Paul's Church and Cwmifor Baptist Chapel. The church and village hall also serve the nearby village of Manordeilo. The village came into existence in the 1820s when the Turnpike road of 1760, which generally followed the old Roman road, was straightened by Thomas Telford.

Cwmisfael (Isfael Vale)

Cwmisfael is a small collection of houses set in a beautiful valley south-west of Llanddarog with a bridge over the Afon y Bantwen, a tributary of the River Gwendraeth Fach.

Cwm-Miles (Miles Valley)

Cwm-Miles is a hamlet on the River Taf in the community of Cilymaenllwyd. The small Independent Chapel was established in 1858 and rebuilt in 1900. The bridge over the River Taf is 18th century and typical of the period with circular holes either side of the main arch, adding strength to the bridge and helping in times of flood. It is Grade II Listed.

Cwmorgan (Shining Valley)

Cwmorgan is a hamlet set in a wooded valley south of Newcastle Emlyn. It has a 19th century former woollen mill, Godremamog Mill, now used as holiday accommodation. The 14ft wheel remains operational and is used to provide electricity.

Cwmpengraig (Valley at the End of the Boulders)

A delightful small village south of Newcastle Emlyn in the valley of the Nant Esgair, it was the site of an 18th century woollen mill and an early 19th century woollen factory with mechanized carding, though willying (the process of cleaning the wool with willow) and spinning remained hand operated.

Cwmtwrch Uchaf (Upper Valley of the Wild Boar)

Cwmtwrch Uchaf or Upper Cwmtwrch is a village split between Carmarthenshire, Powys and Neath Port Talbot. The George IV Inn is in two counties, which has in the past given rise to anomalies with different licensing times applying to different bars. The River Twrch or River Wild Boar is so named after a legend that King Arthur was charged with ridding the area of a pack of wild boars. He is said to have pursued the boars from Dyfed to the western Beacons and threw a large stone at the animals, striking the leader of the pack which fell dead into the river. The legend as told in the Mabinogion however sees the boar, which was really a king transformed into a boar, pursued as far as Cornwall before it was driven into the sea.

Cwmfelin Mynach (Valley of the Monks' Mill)

This lovely little village in the valley of the Afon Gronw was founded by the monks from Whitland Abbey, some time after 1140 when the Abbey was founded, who milled corn here. The housing of the village leading down to the river is 19th century though new housing has been built at the top of the village and one large bungalow on the river bank. Ramoth Baptist Chapel was established around 1775, rebuilt in 1905, with its burial ground opposite. Some 300 yards north-east of the chapel there was a baptistery, where people were baptized in the stream. The steps into the water are still visible.

Older houses in the village were built from local stone which came from quarries to the south-west of the village.

Cwrt y Cadno (Court of Foxes)

Cwrt y Cadno is a scattered community centred on the 1899 Cwrt y Cadno Methodist Chapel, situated on the cross roads in the upper Cothi valley. The route was important for drovers, en route from Cardiganshire to London, as there was water and pasture for the animals.

Cwrt y Cadno's most infamous sons were father and son, Doctors John and Henry Harries. Known as the Wizards of Cwrt y Cadno, they were born at Pantcoy. John Harries was well educated and qualified as a surgeon; indeed he lectured and became a Fellow of the Royal College of Surgeons in Edinburgh. His son, Henry, attended the Royal

College of Surgeons in London before joining his father. The pair certainly gained a wide reputation as being able to heal. They were interested in astrology, but their reputation for wizardry was probably down to the fact that they had a well-stocked library at a time when most households had only the Bible. John died in 1839 and Henry in 1848.

"The sick and sorrowful came to enquire of his oracles from all parts of Wales, and from the testimony of the oldest people in the district, he was eminently successful in his cures. Lunatics were brought to him from parts of Pembrokeshire and Radnorshire, and he had a wonderful power over them. The course of treatment would include what he would term the water treatment, the herbs treatment, and the bleeding treatment. One of his chief methods was, to take the afflicted to the brink of the river, and fire an old flint revolver; this would frighten his patient to such a degree, that he would fall into the pool.

He assumed the power of charming away pain, and was so successful, that people believed thoroughly that he was in league with the evil one. His fame had spread abroad, and Dr. Harries was a very familiar name through the length and breadth of the land. Patients went to him from all parts, some would tramp, and others on horseback over 40 miles to see the 'Doctor'." From *A History of Caio 1904* by Fred S Jones.

On one occasion, John Harries was consulted over the whereabouts of a missing girl. He said that she had been murdered by her sweetheart and buried near a brook where a single tree stood with a bees' nest. The site was duly found and the lover confessed to the murder. Harries was taken before the magistrates at Llandovery charged with abetting the murder. He offered to tell the magistrates the dates of their deaths if they gave him the hour of their birth. He was discharged. He apparently foretold his own death and tried to avoid it by staying in bed on that day because he was to die by accident. The house caught fire and he died falling off a ladder as he tried to dowse the flames. At his funeral it was said that the coffin got lighter as the devil took possession of his body. He is buried at St Cynwyl's in Caio. Records show that Pantcoy burnt down in 1839 but has since been rebuilt.

"Dr. Harries, who lived at Cwrt y Cadno near Pumpsaint, was said to possess a particular book which he kept chained and padlocked. They said that he was even afraid of it himself for he only ventured to open it once every twelve months and always in the presence of another wizard: a schoolmaster from Pencader who occasionally visited him. On a certain day once a year they went out into the woods near Cwrt y Cadno and, after drawing a circle around them, they opened the chained book. Whenever this ceremony was performed it caused thunder and lightning throughout the Vale of Cothi." From *A History of Caio 1904* by Fred S Jones.

Cynghordy

Cynghordy (meaning 'meeting house') is a scattered village in attractive countryside, north of Llandovery with a station on the Heart of Wales Railway. The spectacular Grade II Listed Cynghordy Viaduct carries the Heart of Wales Line above the valley of the River Brân, north of the station at Cynghordy, to the foot of the Sugar Loaf Mountain, on its route from Llandovery to Llanwrtyd Wells. Built by the Llanelly Railway and Docks Company in 1867-1868, it has 18 arches, is 109 feet high and 700 feet long. The railway then goes into a 1,000 yard tunnel. The engineering is particularly impressive as the viaduct curves and rises from one side of the valley to the other.

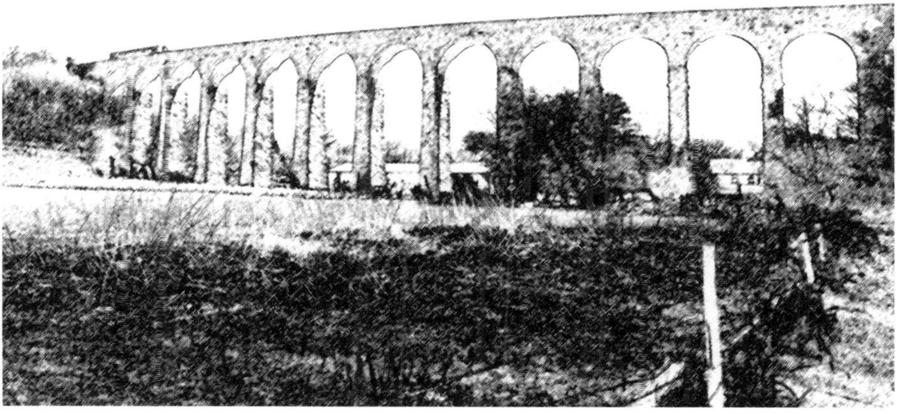

Cynghordy viaduct

Despite having all the elements of a village, including a church, chapel and post office, the elements are so dispersed that there is no sense of a village as such.

Cynheidre (Harvest Farm)

Cynheidre today is an expanding hamlet with a mixture of new and older houses and the Bryn Seion Reformed Congregational Chapel built in 1906. The name goes back to the 16th century, when it was known as Y Gynheydrey.

To many Cynheidre is best known for its colliery, established in 1954 and developed as a 'Super Pit' to extract the anthracite from a massive 196 square miles of deep seams. Four shafts were opened and, in 1972, 1430 miners produced 47200 tons of coal. The seams were at around 200 feet below ground and suffered from methane gas intrusion. The Colliery covered a huge area with shafts 3 and 4 some four miles away and connected by the old Llanelly and Mynydd Mawr Railway. All working at Cynheidre ceased in 1989 and considerable work has been done to remove all above ground evidence of mining.

A new not for profit company, the Llanelli and Mynydd Mawr Railway Company, has been set up to restore and run trains on part of the old railway and an engine shed has been built at Cynheidre with a heritage centre, together with a platform. Eventually there will be a mile of track and a miniature railway. Unfortunately, the major part of the old track has been converted to a cycle way, despite its history of having been the first operating public railway in Britain.

Cynwyl Elfed (Old spelling Conwil Elfed)

Cynwyl Elfed is a parish in the old hundred of Elvet. Situated on the A 484, this village has its origins in Roman times when the area was known as Elvetia. Cynwyl is believed to be formed from 'Cyn': first, and 'gwylio': to watch or guard and means an advanced guard at Elvet. A church was established in the 6th century by St Cynwyl, brother of Deiniol, founder and first Bishop of Bangor. This would appear to shed some doubt as to the interpretation of 'Cynwyl', but the name also appears in Cynwyl Caio.

The church is 14th century in origin, but was renovated on a number of occasions in the 19th century and again in 1903. Originally a chapel of ease under the parish of Abernant, the church was extended in the 16th century with the addition of a second aisle, obviously benefiting from the wealth in the community created by the woollen trade. The local residents obtained an Act of Parliament in 1559 to achieve the change of status from chapel to church.

The village is attractive with white washed and coloured cottages. At the centre is the Blue Bell Inn and behind it the church.

The Afon Duad and Nant Gochen meet in the village, before joining the Gwili just south of the village.

The Elvet Woollen Mill, which was originally powered by the waters of the Duad, is still in production as a commercial operation.

To the east of the village is an Iron Age fort, a cairn and tumulus. John Gorton's *Topographical Dictionary* of 1833 reports a "Druidical Cromlech and open altar and temple. The spa well of Tfosana is well reputed"; Lewis, in 1844, describes the spring as strongly impregnated with iron. He also states that the church was dedicated to St Michael.

Dafen

Dafen is now a suburb of Llanelli with the Prince Philip General Hospital, Dyfed Steel Stockholders and Owens Transport the major employers. The Afon Dafen, from which the village takes its name, flows through Dafen. One theory is that the original name was Taf-ain, meaning spreading water.

Derwydd (Oak Lands)

Derwydd is a small village straddling the A483 between Llandybie and Llandeilo. The village today consists of mainly modern properties. The College Inn provides a focal point.

To the west of the village is Derwydd House. Dating from the 16th century, the property passed into the ownership of Henry Vaughan, a younger brother of John Vaughan, first Earl of Carbery. During the English Civil War, Henry raised a regiment of foot soldiers in support of the King and, in 1643, joined the Royalist forces at Oxford. In gratitude Henry was knighted and raised to the rank of Sergeant Major General. He was sent back to Wales to fight the Parliamentary forces in Pembrokeshire. There is a story that Sir Henry provided the King with cannonballs from his ironworks at Llandyfân, though there is no surviving evidence that a forge existed there at that time. Sir Henry was eventually wounded and captured at the Battle of Naseby and confined to the Tower of London. He was released in 1659 but died the following year. His son, also Henry, was a Lieutenant Colonel and was imprisoned in Denbigh Castle. Henry succeeded his father and died on Christmas Day 1676, after falling from his horse. There is a monument to him in Llandybie church. The house was sold to a private buyer in 1998 and a flat is available for holiday rental, giving access to the main house.

Drefach (Little Town)

Drefach is a village in the Gwendraeth Fawr Valley. A former mining village, the most recent extraction was open cast to the west of the village and this area has now been restored to farmland and a country park. The housing on the hill leading from Cwm Mawr is largely early 20th century with school grounds providing an attractive open feel. The upper part of the village is more modern and the whole village has become an attractive commuter community with good access to Llanelli and Carmarthen.

To the north of Drefach, in trees on private land off the road leading west from the Mansel Arms, lie the ruins of an ancient well chapel, Capel Erbach. The 13th century chapel was built near a spring held to be beneficial in the treatment of spasms. All that remains are the western and southern walls. A mile due west of Capel Erbach stands Capel Begawdin, another ruined well chapel, where the spring rises inside the ruined 13th century chapel. Little seems to be known of the origins of either chapel.

Drefach-Felindre (Little Town-Mill Town)

The villages of Drefach and Felindre expanded and merged into a linked community. The expansion came in the 19th century as the community developed a woollen industry. Early in the 19th century there were four fulling mills with spinning and weaving a cottage industry, but the introduction of power looms saw a major expansion with 24 mills, some employing 100 people, by the early 20th century. The industry declined in the 1920s and all the mills closed. The National Museum of Wales created the National Wool Museum at the Cambrian Mill in 1976.

The village is well served with a central playing field and the Red Dragon community hall. The inn, Tafarn John Y Gwas, is named after a previous landlord, while the Red Lion occupies an old mill.

The church of St Barnabas is 19th century and the oldest chapel in the village; the Unitarian chapel built in 1777 was dismantled in 1952 and rebuilt at the St Fagan's National History Museum. A number of the millworkers' cottages provide a picturesque aspect to these attractive twin villages.

Drefelin

Drefelin (Milltown) is a delightful hamlet set in a wooded valley with picturesque rows of millworkers' cottages. It has two hillside gardens open to the public under the National Gardens Scheme, Pant y Fedwen and Banc y Deri. The Ceridwen Centre is a green holiday, conference, craft and wedding centre on what was Penybanc Farm.

The New Mill occupies a site that has housed a corn mill since 1658 although the present structure is 19th century with all mechanisms

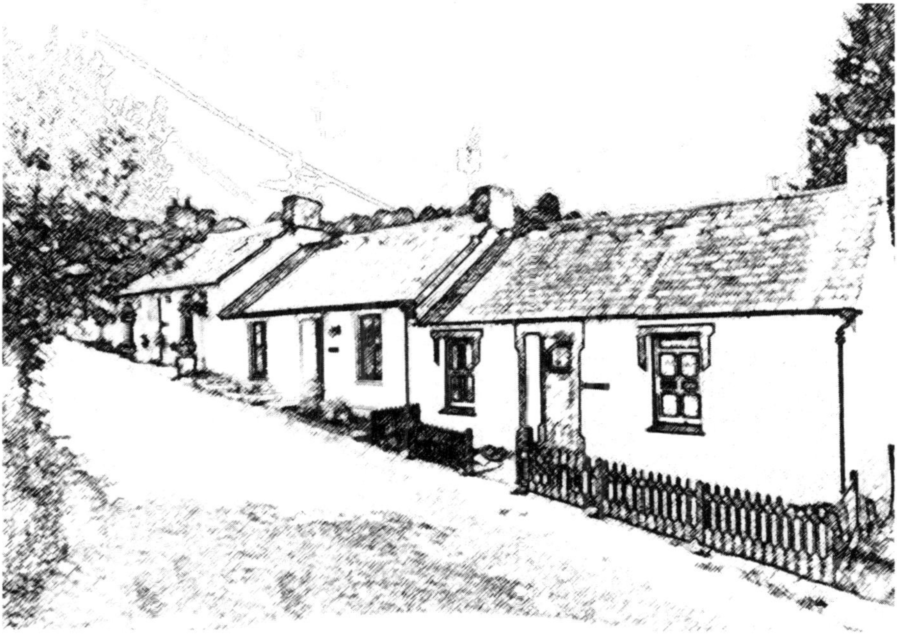

Mill Workers' Cottages, Drefelin

in place. It has been used as an arts exhibition centre. The Nant Bargod provided the power for the village mills.

Dryslwyn (Thicket)

Dryslwyn is dominated by the remains of its castle. Set on a commanding ridge above the River Towy, the castle was relatively late, being developed in the early part of the 13th century before being expanded under Rhys ap Maredudd in the 1280s.

Rhys had supported Edward I in the rebellion of 1282-3 and had been rewarded with new lands. He used his new wealth to extend Dryslwyn and a small town developed on the northern end of the ridge beside the castle. After a series of disputes with the Justicar of South Wales in 1287, Rhys captured the castles of Dinefwr, Carreg Cennen and Llandovery. The response was rapid and an army of 11,000 under the command of the Earl of Cornwall, the King's cousin, laid siege to the castle in August 1287. The siege lasted three weeks and is noted for the collapse of the southern wall, which the attackers were trying to undermine, killing a number of English nobles. Rhys escaped but was captured and executed at York in 1292. The castle was restored, but dismantled early in the 15th century following the rebellion of Owain Glyndwr. Today the castle rewards a strenuous climb with superb views.

The village of Dryslwyn is no more than a collection of houses around a minor cross roads.

The Carmarthen to Llandeilo railway ran through the valley and while the tracks have been removed the level crossing gates remain on the southern side of the Towy.

The old Model Farm of the Cawdor Estate is now the Fig Tree Restaurant, with the Coach House having been converted into a function suite.

Edwinsford

Edwinsford is an estate village on the River Cothi north of Talley. The house dates from 1630 but was subject to major additions. The original house was square with a pyramid roof and central chimney stack. A large wing was added in 1660 and this was extended in 1776 with the addition of a chapel and bellcote. In the 19th century, the chapel was replaced by a ballroom and the bellcote moved across the

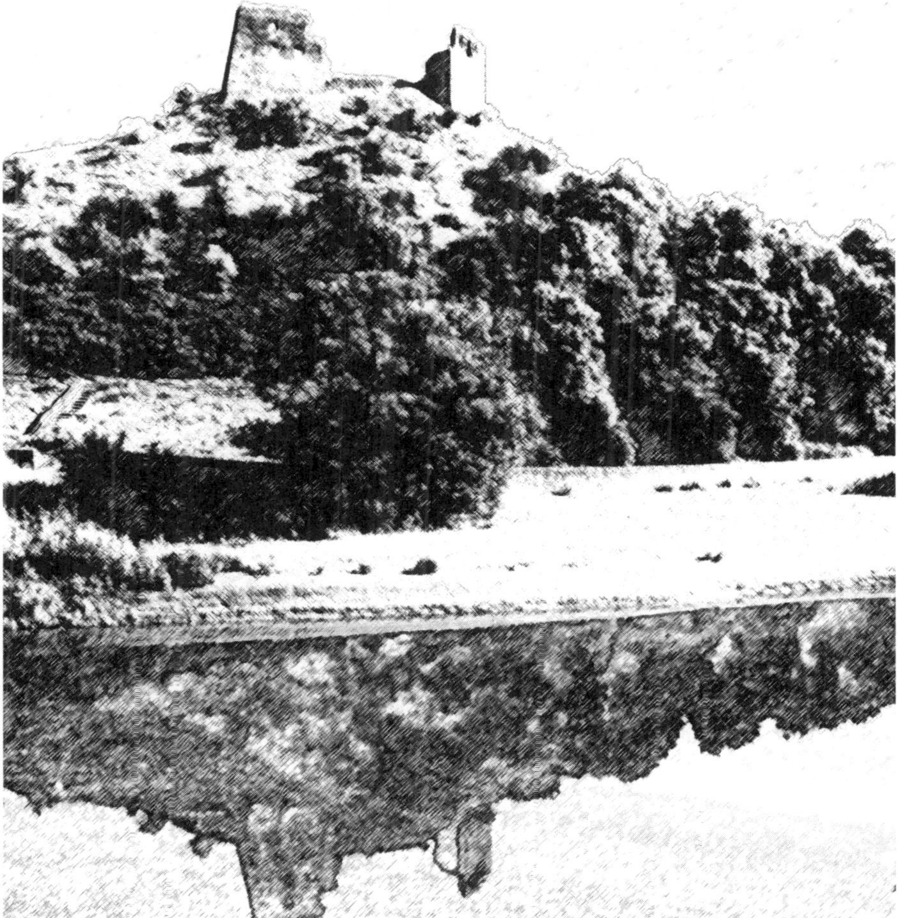

Dryslwyn castle

river to the dairy. The house was closed in the 1930s and quickly fell into a state of decay and is now beyond repair.

The house was built by the Williams family who claimed descent from Hywel Dda. Through marriage they were related to the landed families of the area including the Vaughans of Golden Grove. Further marriages united the estates of Edwinsford with those of Clovelly.

The home farm and dairy were built across the river Cothi from the mansion and now has a holiday cottage giving access to the 350 acre estate and 10 miles of fishing on the Cothi.

Efailwen (White Smithy)

Efailwen is now part of the community of Cilymaenllwyd in the far west of Carmarthenshire. It sits on the A478 Tenby to Cardigan road.

On 13th May 1839 the tollgate at Efailwen was attacked by local farmers who were outraged by the charges for using the turnpike roads at a time of low stock prices. This was the first attack on the toll gates in what was to become known, three years later, as the Rebecca Riots. The Efailwen tollgate was attacked again in June and July of 1839. The rioters dressed in women's clothes and attacked at night. They became known as the Daughters of Rebecca after the reference to Rebecca in the Bible saying "possess the gates of those which hate them". (*Genesis XXIV, 60*)

The riots were short lived but led to a Royal Commission and greater regulation of charges. At the southern end of the village on the A478, before the first house on the right entering the village from the south, is a memorial stone set into the hedge, .

The local café remembers 'Beca' as does the school. Nebo Chapel was established in 1830 and rebuilt in 1860. There are a number of standing stones in the vicinity of Efailwen, but the majority of housing is modern.

Esgairdawe

Meaning ridge of the Tawe, this hamlet north of Llansawel has an Independent Chapel and a few houses, including Esgairdawe Farm. The ridge stands between the valleys of Nant Tawe and the unlikely named Nant Thames, tributaries of the Afon Marlais. The road above the chapel offers fine views to the south.

Eglwys-Cymmyn (St Cynyn's Church)

Alternative spellings: Eglwyscummin, Eglwys-Cymyn, Eglwys Cymmin

Eglwys-Cymmyn is a parish rather than a village that you may have difficulty finding, but St Margaret's Church is well worth the effort. Situated on the B4314 the church sits in a traditional Celtic llan and was originally dedicated to St Cynyn, son of St Cynog and grandson of Brychan, King of Brycheiniog. The present church dates from the 14th century and was built by Sir Guy de Bryan, Lord of Laugharne who claimed descent from St Margaret of Scotland, although the church is dedicated to his niece, St Margaret Marlos, whose tomb is thought to be at nearby Llandawke church.

The church now contains the Avitoria Stone, a 5th century memorial in Latin and Ogham script dedicated to Avitoria and Cunegnus and is unique in being the only Ogham script commemorating a woman. The antiquarian G G T Treherne, who published a history of the church in 1918, was largely responsible for the early 20th century refurbishment of the church and raised money by appealing to every woman in Wales named Margaret to donate a shilling. The stained glass windows date from this time and represent the various saints and noblemen associated with the church. There is a steeply vaulted stone roof though the narrow chancel arch appears to be earlier than the 14th century building. There is a mural of the Ten Commandments written in English and Welsh on the north wall, dating from the 17th century but appearing to have been painted over a medieval depiction of a saint. Normally locked, the key holder lives opposite the church.

Mary Curtis in her 1871 book *The Antiquities of Langharne and Pendine* notes that fairies were active in the parish, especially in a field at Pantread where there were fairy rings, circles of a pea green tint. On entering a ring you would be forced to dance with the fairies until you put a foot outside the ring. It was also the custom in this parish to brew beer for Easter Sunday churchgoers.

Another custom in the parish was to sprinkle salt on a pewter plate and lay it on the deceased in their coffins to ward off evil spirits.

Felindre (Mill Residence)

There are a number of Felindres in Carmarthenshire; as the name would suggest they are not even hamlets. Just outside Llangadog, on the Bethlehem road, Felindre has developed into a sizeable hamlet, separated from Llangadog by the Afon Sawdde, in the middle of open land with Carreg Sawdde Common to the north. A mixture of older and modern housing with roads running to outlying farms and other properties, Felindre was on a road that led, via a ford crossing the Towy, to Manordeilo.

Felinfoel

Felinfoel is now regarded as a suburb of Llanelli, but remains at heart a village. Its name causes some difficulty. Felin is a mill, but 'foel' is the mutated form of Moel, meaning 'bare' or a 'treeless hill' or 'hilltop'. As the village is on the side of a hill, it has been suggested that in this mill the husk was removed before milling so the grain was 'bare'.

The River Lliedi runs through the village which, with a population of 2000, has a wide range of amenities including parks and playing fields, as well as an industrial area.

Perhaps Felinfoel is best known for its brewery and the beers that bear its name. In the 1830s, David John, a local owner of tinplate and iron works bought the King's Head, a coaching inn opposite his house. Next to the inn was a toll gate and with rioters attacking gates, it was decided to change the name to the Union Inn. Like most public houses of the time, the Union brewed its own beers which proved very popular and started to supply other houses. By 1878, demand was such that John erected a new brewery, in his orchard. Its products proved popular, not just with local drinkers, but with farmers who on brewing days collected the spent grain as animal feed. The brewery was built above the River Lliedi and right against the road. With the Union Inn opposite, the road was too narrow for modern traffic and the inn was demolished in 1962. The imposing stone built brewery survives and continues production. It is the oldest brewery in Wales.

Holy Trinity Church, 300 yards from the brewery, was built in 1857 to a design by R K Penson, to relieve pressure on Llanelli parish church. The building was funded by the Nevill family, an important name in the development of Llanelli. The family founded the Llanelli copperworks, owned iron works, mines and shipbuilders. Richard Nevill lived at Felinfoel House and family members are buried in the churchyard. As well as the church the family funded a school in Llanelli where a number of streets bear their name. Felinfoel House was situated opposite Adulam Chapel. It was demolished in 1978 and is now the site of Y Plas care home.

Adulam Chapel was established in 1709 and was the first non-conformist chapel built in the Llanelli area. It was enlarged and later rebuilt and the present building dates from 1852.

Felinfoel was a popular village for the local gentry and industrialists. Ael y Gof was the residence of Sir David Dundas and later his son Sir John. The house was purchased by Edward Nunes Philips in 1868. Edward was manager of the Dafen Tinplate Works owned by Phillips Nunes and Company. He renovated the house and renamed it Ael y Bryn. After the death of his wife in childbirth Edward left for the United States and the house was sold to Earnest Trubshaw who, with his brother-in-law Joseph Smith, started the Western Tinplate Works in Station Road. Earnest's son Harold inherited Caedelyn and Ael y Bryn was to be converted to a school. The outbreak of the World War II saw the house used as a hostel for evacuees and after the war as an old people's home. This was not successful and eventually the house became the Diplomat Hotel. Dundas Lodge at the entrance survives as witness to the past. One notable visitor to the Diplomat was Brian Trubshaw, Concorde test pilot and a descendant of the former owners.

Just to the north of the village the River Lliedi has been dammed twice, in what is known locally as Swiss Valley. It is possible to walk from the park opposite the church through to and around the reservoirs. Very picturesque walks through woodland surrounding the reservoirs provide the village with a tranquil area for relaxation. Running to the west of Felinfoel but through Swiss Valley is a cycle track on what was the bed of the Carmarthenshire Tramroad, later known as the Llanelly and Mynydd Mawr Railway. Established in 1802 by an Act of Parliament, this was the first public railway to operate in Britain. It was established to bring coal from the mining area to the Stradey Ironworks. Motive power was provided by two horses and it was not until 1880 that steam power was used and the line was extended to Cross Hands.

Felingwm Isaf and Felingwm Uchaf (Lower and Upper Mill Valley)

These small, twin mill villages on the Nant Cloidach produced woollen cloth and blankets. Today they are pleasant, tranquil rural villages on the B4310 between Brechfa and Cothi Bridge. The old mill in Felingwm Uchaf is at the bottom of the hill on the Afon Llamarch. The Cloidach and Llamarch meet across the bridge from the mill, with a small weir, a ford and cottages behind, in an idyllic setting. Felingwm Uchaf has the Plough Inn and the little church of St John. The church is situated just over three quarters of a mile north of the village. Built in 1896, it is part of the parish of Llanegwad and is not built on the traditional east-west pattern. Between the village and the church is Felingwm Pottery, established in 1971 it produces majolica, earthenware and bone china.

Felingwm Isaf caters for its residents' spiritual needs with Capel Elim Baptist Chapel situated across the Nant Cloidach from the main road.

Ferryside

Ferryside as its name suggests owes its existence to the ferry that operated between the village and Llansteffan, across the estuary. Giraldus Cambrensis and the Archbishop of Canterbury crossed from here in 1188. The railway from Llanelli to Carmarthen runs between the village and the beach. Cockle fishing was a major source of income but has diminished since the 1990s when the village hit the headlines with gangs of cockle gatherers from Liverpool and the Gower trying to muscle in on the locals. Today the beds are only open at certain times.

Originally there was just a chapel of ease at Ferryside, Capel Llangynheiddon. The village church of St Thomas was built in 1875 as the village, known even then as a bathing resort, expanded. Today, with its rail access to Carmarthen, the village is popular for retirement.

Before the railway, there was no direct road to Carmarthen. The ferry crossed to Llansteffan and the road ran up the western side of the Towy. There was, however, a daily tide boat to Carmarthen commanded by a woman, Admiral Betty, a local character of Amazonian proportions who had been on the station nearly half a century.

Outside the village on the coastal road to the south is the ancient parish church of St Ishmael. There is evidence that there was a village below the church which was destroyed in a storm. Work by the local archaeological society has revealed the remains of a number of stone buildings between the railway and the sea. It is believed that the church was founded in the 6th century by Ishmael who was possibly a nephew of St David. The church does not occupy the typical Welsh llan however. It was extended with the northern aisle and nave being added.

To the north of the village is Iscoed, a substantial property and the home of Sir Thomas Picton. An army officer from the age of 15, Picton went out to the West Indies in 1794 taking part in the capture of St Vincent. He was appointed Governor of Trinidad where he gained a reputation for brutality and torture (the torture known as 'pictoning' is named after him). He returned to Britain and was tried on 35 counts in 1806, but found guilty on only one and was acquitted on retrial. Now a Major General, after service in the Netherlands as Governor of Flushing, Picton joined Wellington in Spain and became celebrated as a successful commander in battle, distinguishing himself at Busaco, the Battle of Fuentes de Onoro, Ciudad Rodrigo, Badajoz and Vittoria. He was honoured by Parliament, became a KB and GCB (Knight of the Order of the Bath and Knight Grand Cross of the Order of the Bath).

In 1815 Picton accepted a high command in the Anglo-Dutch army. He was wounded at Quatre Bras two days before Waterloo, but concealed his injuries and commanded his troops in the battle. Because his luggage had been delayed, he took the field in civilian clothes wearing a top hat. He was killed when a musket ball hit his temple. A monument was erected to his memory in St Paul's Cathedral where his remains were transferred in 1859 by order of Parliament. In Carmarthen the Picton memorial was erected in 1828 following a public subscription, the King contributing 100 Guineas. The monument did not survive the inclement Carmarthen weather and the current monument is much smaller than the original, having been replaced in 1988. some of the bas-reliefs from the original can be seen in the Carmarthen County Museum at Abergwilli. Sir Thomas is the only Welshman buried in St Paul's Cathedral.

Iscoed later became the temporary home of John Simmons Tregoning II, manager and, on the death of his father, owner of the Morfa Tinplate works in Llanelli, before he moved to Portiscliff, a house to the south of Ferryside. (Portiscliff was the former home of Rear Admiral Charles Hamlyn Williams, the younger son of Sir James Hamlyn-Williams of Edwinsford.) He travelled to work daily on the train from Ferryside. He was known for his paternalistic approach to his workforce, employing a doctor and setting up a sickness and disability fund. He constructed homes for the workforce that remain occupied today in Cornish Place and Campbell Street, Llanelli. He became Chairman of Carmarthenshire County Council in 1896.

The sad demise of Iscoed Mansion started after World War II when it was divided into flats for people awaiting council housing. The lead was stripped from the roof and the building was vandalised to the extent that all but the south wing was a ruin.

Tregoning Hill to the south of the village was given to the National Trust by the descendants of John Simmons Tregoning II in 1962.

Ffairfach (Little Mary)

Ffairfach, a village on the southern side of the Towy from Llandeilo, is now a dormitory suburb for Llandeilo and other towns. It used to have two railway stations; though the line from Carmarthen, which passed through the village behind the Tregib Inn, is no longer in existence.

The Union Poor House serving the Llandeilo area was built at Ffairfach in 1839 and was taken over by the local authority in 1930 and has since been demolished.

One remnant of the past is the village pump near the Torbay Inn. Until the early noughties, it still dispensed crystal clear water. The old pump disappeared and, while replaced, is no longer connected to the spring.

Ffaldybrenin (King's Pound)

A small community centred on a large chapel, built in 1833, and graveyard to the north of the A482 Pumsaint to Lampeter road

Ffarmers

Ffarmers is a small village with a mixture of new and old houses, north of the A482 Pumsaint to Lampeter road. Originally named after the long closed Farmers Arms, the centre has some 50 houses, a community owned village pub, the Drovers' Arms, and a village hall. Sarn Helen, the Roman road from south to north Wales runs through the village and, as the name of the pub indicates, it was a stop on an old drove route. There is evidence of a 15th century fulling mill on the River Twrch which runs past the village. Unusually, the village has no chapel or church though there are a number of chapels nearby as well as Llanycrwys church.

The surrounding area is agricultural, with small hedge lined fields to the north and west while towards the north-east the land rises towards the Cambrian Mountains, offering superb views.

In the late 1960s and early 1970s the village became home to the neo-pagan Selene Community. Based at Can-y-Lloer, Song of the

Moon, the leader Tony Kelly and his two wives shocked villagers by wandering round the fields in the nude. They lived on benefits and produced a magazine called *Communes* acting as an information source for hippies, pagans and alternative communities throughout Britain. The community numbers dropped from 34 to 3 and with the magazine in financial difficulties the Selene Community failed.

Five Roads

Situated on the B4309 Llanelli to Carmarthen road, the name reflects the meeting of five roads at this point. A growing community with the majority of housing being modern, Five Roads has a pub and Post Office but the only chapel, Rehoboth, lies over a mile from the junction, on Heol Rehoboth. The Stag and Pheasant, now renamed the Stag, was a meeting place for the Rebecca Rioters in1843, a piece of history recorded on a Blue Plaque at the Stag.

Foelgastell

Foelgastell is a ribbon development on the road from Cefneithin to Porthyrhyd, parallel to the A48 dual carriageway. The name means hilltop stronghold, but there is no evidence of any fortification though a dilapidated farm known as Caerllwyn, some 660 yards west of the village, gives further evidence of some fortified position. The village has expanded considerably with new housing, but within the older central area is the Smith's Arms. Peniel Calvinistic Methodist chapel lies at the south-eastern entrance to the village.

Furnace

Furnace is now to all intents and purposes a suburb of Llanelli, but its origins lie in the furnace that was established on the Stradey Park estate in the 1750s. The furnace was taken over by Alexander Raby, a London ironmaster, in 1795 and a village developed around the works, taking on the name Furnace.

Raby occupied Furnace House until his finances failed. The house later became the home of Sir John Cowell Stepney who renamed it The Dell. The house has since been demolished.

Alexander Raby's son Arthur lived at Caemawr Cottage, described as a thatched wooden chateau, until it burnt down in 1824. Alexander

Raby junior lived at Bryn Môr which eventually became the basis for the Stradey Park Hotel, the four star hotel which offers superb views over Llanelli.

100 yards north of the hotel are the remains of Raby's blast furnace, hidden amongst the trees of the Dingle. Raby produced cannon and cannonballs for the Board of Ordnance during the Napoleonic Wars. The Mynydd Mawr Railway, the first operating public railway, was used to bring coal down the valley. The furnace is a Grade II listed monument.

Today Furnace is a combination of 19th century terraced housing and, on higher ground, modern housing.

Garnant (Wild Stream)

Garnant is a village born from the coal and tinplate industries in the Aman valley. As with Glanaman, it was given its name to identify the railway station when the line opened in 1840.

In the early part of the 20th century there were six major coal mines in Garnant and a tin plate works. The village saw a major expansion in housing, shops, chapels and churches. The Amman Tinplate works closed in 1932 and mining on any large scale ceased in 1935 with the closure of the Raven Colliery. Between 1987 and 1992 an open cast mine on the southern side of the valley was active. The village has been transformed over the last 20 years. The open cast mining area is now an 18 hole golf course with a clubhouse offering superb views across the valley. The rivers which were once heavily polluted are now clean, with a riverside walk and cycle path. Where the Amman Tinplate works once stood is a park.

The chapels in Garnant remain, as does Christchurch at the bottom of the Twyn. Christchurch was built in 1842 by Morgan Morgan of Ty Llwyd, Glanaman to a design by Robert Ebbels, an architect specialising in church design. Ebbels was responsible for a number of churches in his home region around Wolverhampton as well as Surrey and the Isle of Wight. The pubs are down to two, but the saddest site in the village is the Workmen's Hall. Built in 1927 with contributions from both miners and mine-owners just a year after the bitter General Strike, it had seating for 915 and a stage capable of accommodating the largest choirs and theatrical productions. The hall closed in 1972, to be reopened as a leisure centre in 1985. Its more recent history as a cannabis factory is a sad reflection on its past.

Trains started running again on the railway line in 2011, carrying coal from the open cast site at Tairgwaith, further up the valley. Longer term it is hoped to start running passenger trains again.

Gelli Aur (Golden Grove)

Gelli Aur was the estate village to the Golden Grove mansion. It is in the parish of Llanfiangel Aberbythych, or St Michael's at the Mouth of the Bythych, a stream that joins the Towy. The church was erected in 1617 and rebuilt around 1850 at the expense of Lord Cawdor to a design by Sir Gilbert Scott, architect of the Albert Memorial, who was also responsible for work at Llandybie.

Gelli Aur Country Park offers 60 acres of peaceful park and woodland on the southern side of the Towy opposite Aberglasney. Originally the home of the Vaughan family, Golden Grove passed to the Cawdors in 1804. Probably the largest house in the valley, it is closed to the public but the parkland is open (no entry charge but pay and display parking is in operation).

Golden Grove mansion was rebuilt by the Earl of Cawdor between 1827 and 1832, replacing the Tudor mansion of the Vaughan family which was situated to the north-west of the new house at a lower level. The remains of the old house became a walled garden and the lake that adjoined it remains. The new house presented much better views over the valley.

The Vaughan family name in Welsh was Fychan. Gruffydd Fychan was married to Katherine, daughter of Maredudd ap Tudor. Their son Hugh Fychan moved to Carmarthenshire in 1485 and married Jane, daughter of Morris ab Owain, Steward of the Lordship of Kidwelly and Receiver of the Commotes of Iscennen and Carnwyllion. Hugh Fychan was appointed Forester of Kidwelly and by 1492 was Gentleman Usher at the court of Henry VII, his cousin. In 1532 Hugh Fychan, or Vaughan as he was now known, was appointed Keeper and Receiver of lands in Kidwelly confiscated by Henry VIII from Rhys ap Gruffydd of Dinefwr. The family home was Cwrt Bryn y Beirdd, a 14th century unfortified mansion opposite Carreg Cennen Castle, in the Commote of Iscennen. Hugh and Jane had one son, John Vaughan.

John Vaughan of Kidwelly moved to Gelli Aur in the 16th century. His son Walter married twice, first into the Dinefwr family and then to Letitia, daughter of Sir John Perrot of Laugharne. Walter's eldest son John (1572-1634) was twice Member of Parliament for

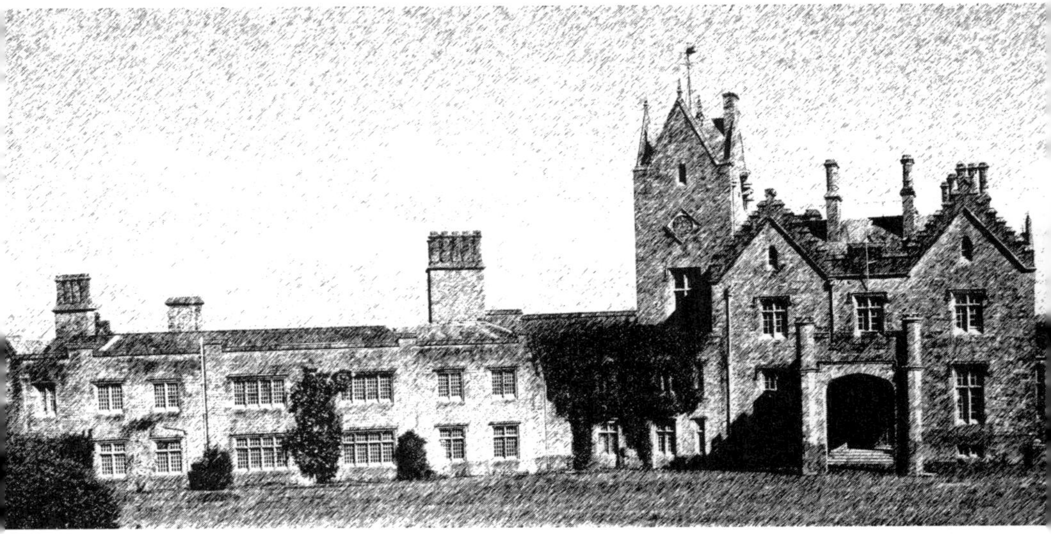

Golden Grove mansion

Carmarthen Borough. He served under the Earl of Essex in Ireland and subsequently was appointed to the household of Prince Charles. He was created Baron Mulingar in 1621 and Earl of Carbery in 1628.

His son Richard succeeded him as 2nd Earl of Carbery and became Lord President of the Marches of Wales and was created Baron Vaughan of Emlyn (a British rather than an Irish peerage) A royalist in the early years of the Civil War, he took no part in hostilities after 1644. A refugee at Golden Grove during that war was Jeremy Taylor whose religious writings include *Golden Grove; or a Manuall of daily prayers and letanies.* At the time of his death Richard Vaughan owned 50,000 acres in Wales as well as land in Ireland.

The 3rd and last Earl of Carbery was Richard's son John (1640-1713). Like his father and grandfather he was Member of Parliament for Carmarthen Borough but was also appointed Governor of Jamaica 1674-78, where his deputy was the notorious Sir Henry Morgan. He returned to London and became President of the Royal Society 1686-89. He was described by Samuel Pepys as "one of the lewdest fellows of the age". His only daughter married Lord Bolton but died without issue and the estate passed to a cousin, yet another John Vaughan (1693-1765). He built a new Golden Grove mansion alongside the original that had been destroyed by fire in 1729. His grandson, John Vaughan (1757-1804) died without issue and left the estate to his friend John Campbell, Lord Cawdor. The Campbell family already owned land in Pembrokeshire as well as Cawdor Castle in Scotland. John Campbell's son, John Frederick Campbell, second Baron Cawdor was created Earl of Cawdor in 1827. It was he who built the present Golden Grove mansion. During World War II the house was taken over by the United States Air Force. John Duncan Vaughan Campbell, 5th Earl of Cawdor (1900-1970) spent most of his time in Scotland and leased Golden Grove mansion and the surrounding land to Carmarthenshire County Council. The bulk of the estate is used as an agricultural college.

In 1606 the Court of Great Sessions, the main court for the prosecution of major misdemeanours was held at Golden Grove because the plague was present in Carmarthen.

The Cawdor name is continued in the area in the Cawdor, a leading hotel in Llandeilo. The Cawdor Hotel was formerly the Bear Inn, described by Sir Richard Hoare in the 1790s as the "worst in South Wales" and by a Miss Spence as "very uncomfortable and exorbitant", but was commended by *The Cambrian Travellers' Guide and Handbook* of 1808.

The Arboretum at Gelli Aur has a selection of specimen trees from around the world. It was planted in the 1860s in parkland that already contained a range of mature oaks and sweet chestnuts.

The Deer Park at Gelli Aur has some 20 Fallow deer in its 20 acres. The original Deer Park was some twenty times larger with a herd of up to 600 deer. Today the deer can be seen from the terrace of the café where there is a resident peacock.

Gelliwen (White Wood)

A hamlet in the parish of Tre-lech ar Betws, north-west of Meidrim. A collection of houses in the beautiful, tranquil tree lined valley of the Afon Cynin, with Ainon Baptist Chapel, built 1828 and rebuilt in 1880.

Glanaman (Banks of the Aman)

Before the industrialization of the Aman Valley, there was no such village. The valley known now, as then, as Cwmaman was a remote and wild area with scattered farms using limestone and coal for agricultural and domestic purposes. The residents had the reputation of being lawless and butchers from Cwmaman, who had stalls in Swansea Market, "on a Saturday night, after selling their meat, would drink until the following Sunday morning. Many of the older people swore that one endangered one's life by venturing out onto the streets on a Saturday paying out night, when the butchers had closed their stalls, for there would be many drunken and malicious louts always ready to set upon anybody who went too close to them, both in the town and the outlying villages" (*Hanes Eglwysi Annibynnol Cymru*, J Thomas, & T Rees, Liverpool, 1872, Vol. II, p. 40.)

Indeed so bad was the reputation of the valley people that the following rhyme was popular in Swansea:

All men in Cwmamman born,
You are each one the Devil's spawn.
Repent most quickly you must do
Or he will take you, two by two.

There was also the allegation that the custom of 'sin eating' was carried on in the valley. A plate of salt was placed on the chest of a dead man and covered with a piece of bread. The sins of the deceased were believed to pass to the person who ate the bread and salt and a vagabond was given sixpence to take on the sins. The practice was not uncommon in the 17th century in England, Ireland, Scotland and Germany, but when the suggestion was made that it was still carried on in the valley in a book published in 1881 there was an outcry.

The first non-conformist chapel was built in 1773 high on the side of the valley alongside the old Neath to Llandeilo road. The Chapel, Hen Bethel, is no longer in regular use and showing signs of decay though at 6 a.m. on Christmas morning a service is held there.

The nature of the valley changed in 1817 with the advent of the Neath to Cross Inn (Ammanford) Turnpike Road. The Cross Keys Inn marks the site of the old Turnpike Gate. The Railway followed in 1840 bringing with it the names of Glanamman and Garnant (the spelling later changed to the Welsh form Glanaman). Coal mining and tin plate works saw the industrialization of the valley and a rapid increase in population. The valley quickly became industrialised with coal mines taking advantage of the rich anthracite seams. Glanaman had the Raven Tinplate Works which had closed by 1936 and is now the site of a council depot. The raven was the crest of the Dinefwr family who owned much of the valley.

A stone bridge over the Aman was built in the early 1800s probably by Morgan Morgan of Ty Llwyd, Glanaman, who also built Christchurch in Garnant. The bridge contains the circular holes, pioneered by William Edwards, builder of the old bridge at Pontypridd, designed to strengthen the main arch of the bridge, but in this case they are smaller and nearer the main arch than those of Edwards and his son. The bridge was widened in 1935 and the old and new parts can be seen beneath the bridge.

Possibly the most prominent figure in Glanaman in the early years of the 20th century was Henry Folland. He lost an arm at an early age but worked as an assistant cashier at the Raven Tinplate Works. In 1901, at the age of 23 he was promoted to assistant manager and became manager and then director, creating the Folland Group that owned 11 works in the area. The Folland Group merged with Richard Thomas & Baldwin.

The cottage hospital was opened in Glanaman in 1936 in the former home of Mr and Mrs Henry Folland. Mrs Folland donated their house, Frondeg, and paid for the medical instruments and part funded the running of the hospital. Horny Road was renamed Folland Road after her.

Chapels were built to meet the demands of the growing population and the most beautiful of these was Brynseion, completed in 1912 and Grade II Listed for the "richness of the chapel architecture, associated with the prosperity of local coal and tinplate industries before 1914". Sadly the chapel is now closed and vandals and the elements are taking their toll. St Margaret's Church was opened in 1933, replacing an earlier corrugated metal building that had been used since 1907. Services ceased in 2008.

Little can be seen of the industrial past of the village. Forestry has taken over the southern side of the valley with its attractive walks, while the river, now virtually pollution free, is used by fishermen and the tree lined banks have a riverside walk. One relic of the past, however, is visible in the form of a truck which ran out of control and ended in the river.

Glandy Cross

A hamlet on the A478 Tenby to Cardigan road named after nearby Glandy Farm. There has been significant development of modern housing along the main road and the Maencluchog to Llanglydwen road. The Cross Inn is a small pub listed in the heritage interiors CAMRA Guide.

Thfe main interest in and around Glandy Cross is the complex of Neolithic and bronze age features, forming one of the largest prehistoric settlements in western Britain. These include the Meini Gwyr stone circle, ring cairns, round barrows and standing stones, as well as two hill forts. The easiest to visit is Meini Gwyr which is in a field next to the final bungalow on the left on the Maenclochog road. Only two of the seventeen stones remain but the raised circle is visible and there is a weather worn, informative notice at the gate. In the garden of the Bluestone Motor Services is a replica stone circle.

Gorslas (Green Bog)

Gorslas is an old mining village between Llandeilo and Cross Hands. In the 1820s there were the Gilfach, Millers, George and Pwllylledrim pits here with coal being transported to Llanelli by a tram road built by Alexander Raby in 1805.

Just outside the village are traces of Castell y Rhingell, believed by some to be the castle called Lychewein, of Welsh folklore.

Above the village is the Llyn Llech Owain nature reserve and country park. Some confusion relates to the identity of Owain, some suggesting that it was Owain Glyndwr, others that it was Sir Owain, a knight of the Round Table while others simply identify him as a well keeper. The story, however, is similar: that he forgot to replace the stone cap on the well and the water flooded out. Realizing his error, he rode his horse around the flood three times, marking the limit of the lake.

In reality the lake is glacial in origin and until the 1990s was used to supply water to the surrounding area.

Gwernogle (Place of Alders)

Gwernogle is a hamlet set in beautiful countryside north of Brechfa. The small cluster of houses is centred around the 1750 Independent Chapel. Capel Farm, however, refers to a much older chapel in Gwernogle. St Silyn was a hermit who lived here and a chapel of ease was built on the site of his cell. The chapel was described as in ruins in a report of 1715. In 1902 the Reverend Owen of Llanfihangel Rhos y Corn opened Eglwys Zinc as a Mission Church. This zinc building survived as a church until 1960 when it was deconsecrated and sold to the Young Farmers Club for £20.

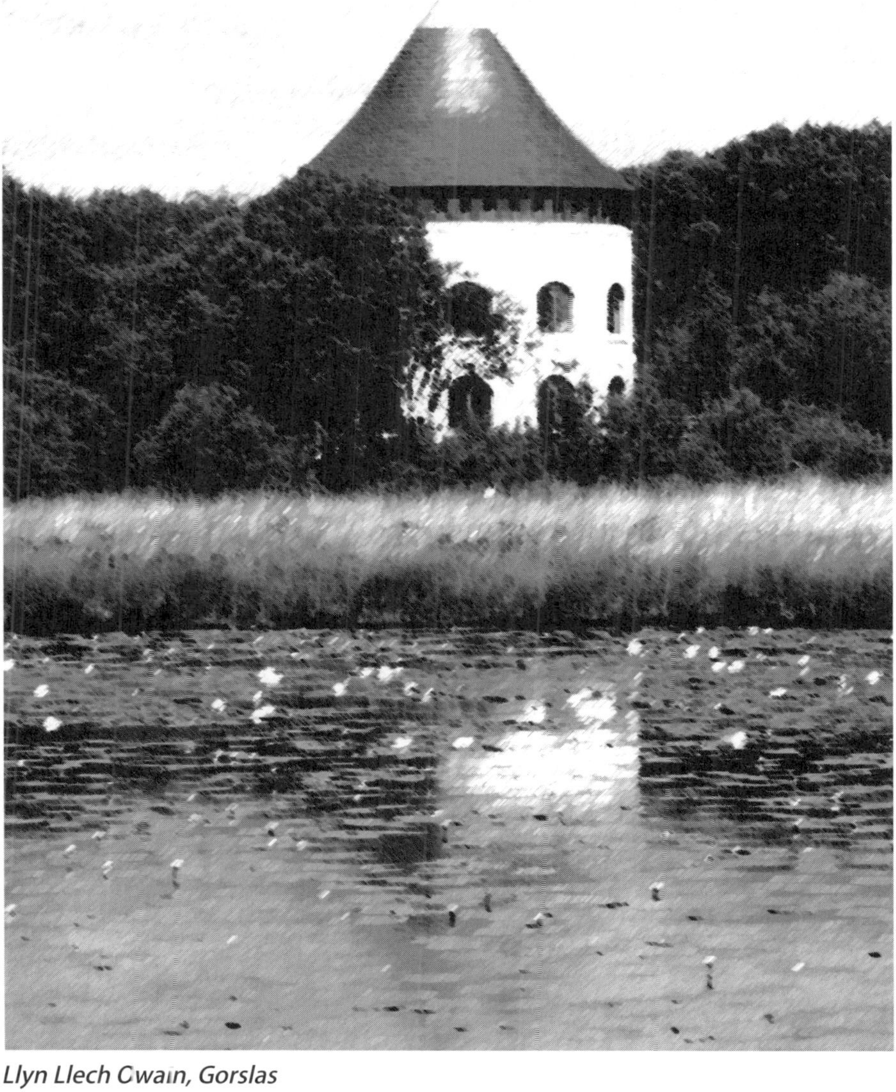

Llyn Llech Owain, Gorslas

Gwyddgrug (Conspicuous Hill)

A small village on the A485 with an Independent Chapel built in 1895. The road crosses the Afon Gwyddgrug.

Gwynfe (Holy)

Gwynfe or Capel Gwynfe, Carmarthenshire's Village of the Year in 2004, is a scattered collection of farms and houses west of the Llangadog to Brynaman road. The Chapel of Ease under Llangadog is now the church hall and the later All Saints Church was built in 1898. An outline of a wall may be evidence that there was a Celtic llan on this site. The village community hall is adjacent to the church and was built in 2004.

Harford

Harford is a hamlet on the A482 Llanwrda to Lampeter road. It is a small community scattered along the main road. There is a garage and a caravan and camping site offering fishing. Harford was named after John Harford of the Bristol based Harford Bank. While his home was at Blaise Castle, Bristol, he acquired land in Carmarthenshire and Cardiganshire early in the 19th century. He was a friend of the Bishop of St David's, Bishop Burgess, and donated the land he owned in Lampeter to enable the establishment of Wales' first University, St David's College Lampeter, the oldest university in England and Wales after Oxford and Cambridge. He built a mansion, Falcondale, on the outskirts of Lampeter but Blaise Castle continued as his main residence. Falcondale is now a hotel.

Hebron

Hebron is a hamlet in the north-west of the county on the Pembrokeshire border. The Independent Chapel of Hebron was built in 1805. The chapel stands some 100 feet above the river on the west side of the River Taf.

Hendy (Old House)

Hendy grew up as an industrial village on the borders of Carmarthenshire and Glamorgan, west of Pontardulais. A tin plate works was established in 1870 and the owners built forty houses to accommodate the workforce. Other workers built their own houses and Hendy became a sizeable village.

The village today is on the link road from the M4 Motorway to Pontardulais. The village has an industrial estate and a considerable amount of new housing to the north of Iscoed Road. It is well served with its cricket ground and sports facilities at Hendy Park. The church of St David was built in 1986, replacing a building of 1902, and has some beautiful stained glass.

Henllan (Old Church)

Henllan (Old Church) is a village in Cardiganshire though the parish stretches south of the Teifi into Carmarthenshire. The Teifi passes through a tree lined gorge near Henllan. Today it is the terminus for the Teifi Valley steam railway. Originally part of the Carmarthen to Newcastle Emlyn line, the track is now narrow gauge.

During World War II the village housed 1,200 Italian prisoners of war. To cater for their religious needs they were allowed to use one hut as a church. One of the prisoners, 21-year-old Mario Ferlito, painted a fresco and murals. Empty tins were used to create candlesticks and the paint for the murals and fresco was made from fruit and vegetables, tea leaves mixed with a paste made from fish bones and pickling fluid. The Church of the Sacred Heart was the result and is still used for masses.

Henllan Amgoed – see Henllanfallteg

Henllanfallteg (The old church of St Mallteg)

In the west of the county, Henllanfallteg takes in the villages and hamlets of Llanfallteg, Henllan Amgoed, Cwmfelin Boeth, Hiraeth and Rhydywrach. The population of this large area is under 500. Henllan Amgoed, Cwmfelin Boeth, and Rhydywrach are small collections of houses near large farms, while Hiraeth is a cross roads.

St Mallteg's Church, now redundant and sold, is located in the midst of Llanfallteg Farm in Llanfallteg West, which basically consists of the farm, church and Llanfallteg House. St Mallteg is a saint about whom nothing is known other than that his festival was November 1st.

At Llanfallteg village hall is a replica of a stone, found at Castell Dwyran Chapel; it is known as the Vortipor Stone and dates from 540. The original is in the Carmarthen County Museum and there are inscriptions in Ogham and Latin. The inscription reads 'Memoria Voteporigis Protictoris' or 'In Memory of Voteporigis Protector'. There is some dispute as to whether the stone relates to Vortiporius because of the lack of the 'r', but he was King of Dyfed, of Irish descent, prior to 540. Castell Dwyran is no longer, indeed there is no evidence of a castle, but the ruined chapel of ease on the site was a small crudiform structure. It sits in the middle of a farm south of Llanfallteg across the border in Pembrokeshire.

The Plash Inn (plash is an old form of splash) made the headlines in 2009 when it was offered as the prize in its own online pub quiz. Outside is one of two village pumps. The River Taf flows through the village and divides Llanfallteg from Llanfallteg West, which used to be in Pembrokeshire.

There has been an expansion of new housing in recent years but little to spoil the essential rural nature of the area.

To the west of Cwmfelin Boeth is the little ruined church of St Canna and St Canna's Seat. The seat is inscribed and has a hollow. It was situated next to the church where there was a holy well. A ritual involving throwing pins into the well and then sitting on the stone was claimed to cure ague and intestinal complaints.

St David's Church in Henllan Amgoed (Old Church in the Trees) is another redundant church in this community. It is situated near Henllan Farm and has now been sold. Henllan Independent Chapel was important in the spread of non-conformity in the area, with no fewer than ten chapels being set up from there in the late 17th century. Although the chapel was not built until 1696, there was a large group of worshippers meeting in private houses with a full time pastor from the 1770s.

Hiraeth – see Henllanfallteg

Horeb

Horeb is a quiet small village in rural surroundings, half a mile away from Five Roads, north of Llanelli. It takes its name from its chapel. The village inn is named the Waun Wyllt (Wild Moor). It is in the valley of the Afon Liedi and the old Mynydd Mawr tram road, now a cycle track, passes to the east of the village. The village has a mixture of new and older housing.

Idole

Idole is a modern commuting village mainly of bungalows off the A484 Carmarthen to Kidwelly road. Its name however is anything but modern. In post Norman Carmarthenshire the county was divided into commotes and the commote of Cydwelli was divided into administrative areas, one of which was Iscoed. Iscoed was further divided into ten cow units (vaccae). One of these was Vaccae Ithole, giving the modern name Idole. The purpose of the vaccae was to raise tax to pay for the maintenance of law and order and the tenants of each vaccae had to pay five shillings (the price of a cow) on May 1st every third year.

Johnstown

Johnstown was described by Thomas Morgan in his 1912 edition of *The Place Names of Wales* as a small village. Situated on the Carmarthen to Llansteffan road, it is now little more than a sprawling suburb of Carmarthen, with housing estates, schools, leisure and sports facilities and factories.

The village was named after John Jones of Ystrad, a colourful barrister and politician. Jones was born in King Street, Carmarthen in 1777. His father was agent to the Vaughan estate of Golden Grove (Gelli Aur), which had passed from the Vaughans to the Earl of Cawdor in 1804. Jones was educated at Eton and Christchurch College, Oxford and was called to the Bar in 1803.

His early political history gives an insight into the influence of, and rivalry between, the local landed families. Jones, a Tory, was supported by Lord Dinefwr but opposed by the Whig Earl of Cawdor. He entered Parliament in 1815 for Pembroke Boroughs, but by agreement gave it up in 1818. He challenged John Frederick Campbell, heir to Lord Cawdor, for the Carmarthen seat in 1820 but held back for fear of causing a backlash against Dinefwr's son George Rice in the Carmarthenshire seat. He was however elected for Carmarthen a year later when Campbell succeeded his father.

He was an active politician, campaigning on many local issues and, although a Welsh speaker, he regretted the fact that charity schools "afforded the means of perpetuating the language which was before greatly in decline". His views on the Welsh language did not, however, stop him from giving Carmarthen's Welsh language St David's church financial support. He failed in various attempts to gain a paid government post, turning down the one offer to become a judge in India.

1831 proved an eventful year. Jones was injured in rioting during the election in Carmarthen, which had to be postponed. He then fought a duel with the defeated candidate for Pembrokeshire, Robert Fulke Greville, before being re-elected in the August re-run of the election. He lost the election for the new seat of Carmarthen and Llanelly in 1832 but was elected as a Conservative for the Carmarthenshire seat in 1837, which he held until his death in 1842.

At his funeral at St Peter's, the *Carmarthen Journal* reported that he had been described as having had "probably the greatest influence of any private gentleman in the Principality". After his death it was discovered that his estate was insolvent and his bequests to his sister and natural son were worthless.

Llanarthney

Llanarthney is a village on the B4300 that runs from Llandeilo to Carmarthen on the southern side of the River Towy. The origins of the village date back at least as far as the 6th century when a church was established, dedicated to St Arthney (possibly Arthen, a son of King Brychan of Brycheiniog). In the late 11th and early 12th century a new church dedicated to St David was consecrated by Herewald, Bishop of Llandaff. Despite its Celtic origins, the llan is not the usual circular area. The description in 1844 was: "The church, dedicated to St David, is a neat plain edifice, with a low square tower, but presents no architectural details of importance" (From *A Topographical Dictionary of Wales* (S Lewis, 1844)).

Saron Chapel, just out of the village towards Llandeilo, is one of only two chapels in Wales to have a family coat of arms displayed above its front door. (The other is Smyrna Baptist Chapel, Porthyrhyd, Cilycwm.) Land for the chapel and burial ground was donated by Edward Abadan of Middleton Hall on condition that his family coat of arms was displayed and that the congregation remembered the family in their prayers.

The village retains its pub, the Emlyn Arms, formerly the Paxton, just across the bridge, over the Afon Gwynon, from the church.

The railway from Abergwilli Junction to Llandeilo was opened to goods trains in 1864, and passengers a year later, with a station for Llanarthney. The line was built on the Towy flood plain and was subject to frequent flooding. It closed in September 1963. The line is still visible to the north of the church.

The parish extends over the hill to the south and includes the former Middleton Hall estate, now the National Botanic Garden of Wales. Standing out above the valley is Paxton's Tower, sometimes known as Nelson's Tower.

The Middleton or Myddelton (Middleton was used in Carmarthenshire but Myddelton in London) family of Denbigh built a mansion on the site in the early 1600s. David Middleton, the first owner, was the brother of Sir Hugh Myddelton who was responsible for the construction of the New River, which supplied London with clean water. Completed in 1613, it brought water from Ware in Hertfordshire to Clerkenwell. By following the 100ft contour the canal was 37 miles long and fed a number of reservoirs. Hugh Myddelton was an MP, a rich entrepreneur, mine owner and jeweller to King James I. As a private enterprise, water was supplied only to those who paid the 26 shillings a year charge. The King himself owned half the company. Thomas Myddelton, another brother, was Lord Mayor of London, in 1613, and attended the first release of water. The New River Company became very profitable and by 1700 a single share paid £200 a year. The system is still in use today. In 1827 Myddelton Square, London EC1was built and named after Sir Hugh Myddelton

In 1789 William Paxton purchased the estate, converted the Hall into the Home Farm and built a new hall, regarded as one of the most splendid mansions in South Wales. He also created a water park and, using elevated reservoirs, equipped the house with water closets. Paxton, a Scotsman, had started his career in the Navy but moved to India where he turned to banking, eventually establishing a merchant bank. Standing for Parliament for Carmarthen, he promised to build a bridge over the Towy but, following a false rumour that he was about to be bankrupt, he lost the election. In 1802, in what was called the 'Pig and Swill Election', he spent £15,690 in entertaining the electors, but still lost. A friend of Nelson, he had Nelson's Tower otherwise known as Paxton's Tower built in his memory, using the money he had set aside for the building of the bridge. Originally a track led from the hall to the tower and carriages would transport guests to the tower where the first floor was a dining room with magnificent views over the Towy

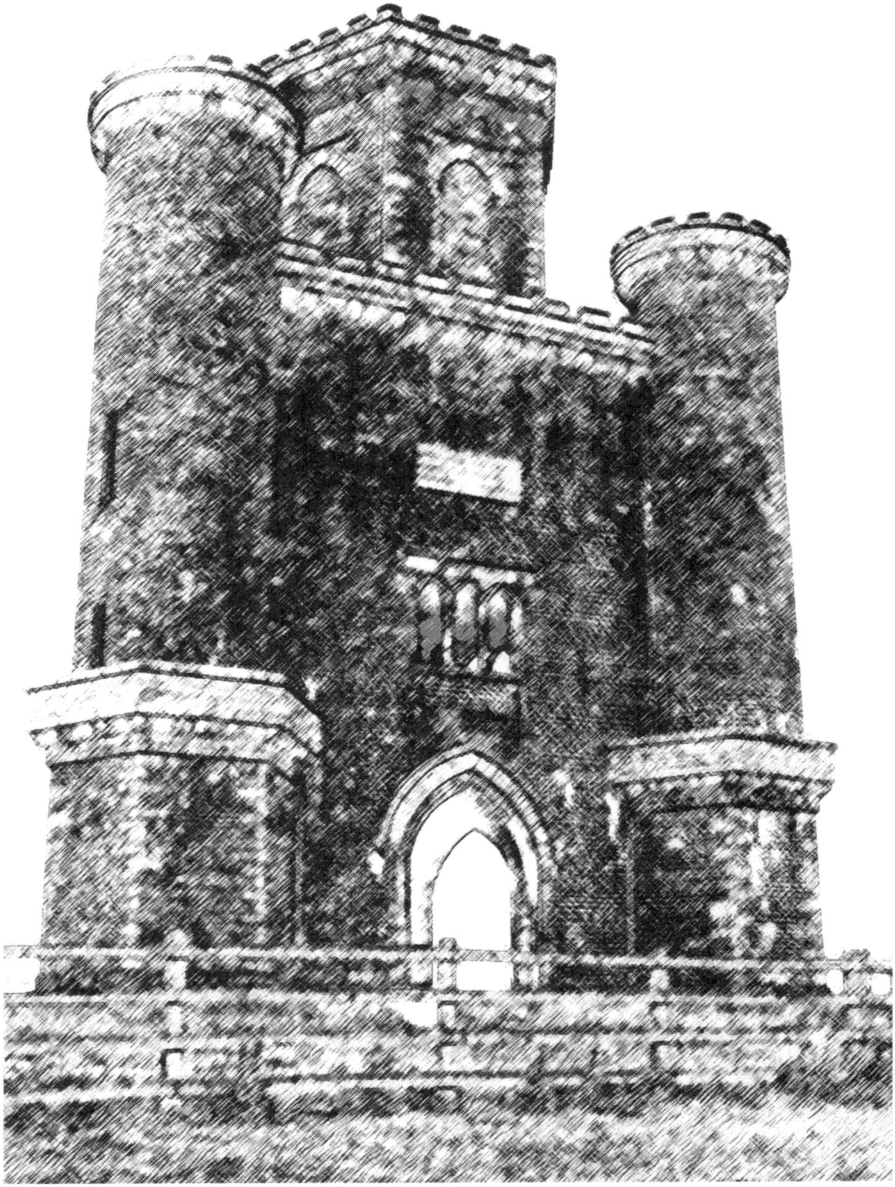

Paxton's or Nelson's Tower, Llanarthney

valley. The architect for the hall and the tower was S P Cockerell, a descendant of Samuel Pepys the 17th century diarist. An early visitor described the tower as having a "lofty and sumptuous banqueting room" and, on the second floor, an "apartment designed for a prospect room": one window was of painted glass consisting of a portrait of the hero, the cockpit scene presenting him in his last moments and "the emblematical representation of his ascent to immortality".

Paxton died in 1824 and the hall and estate was sold to Edward Adams who had made his fortune in Jamaica. His son, also Edward Adams changed the family name to Abadam, giving the name to the Abadam Arms at Porthyrhyd. The property changed hands over the years but the house was gutted by fire in 1931. The outline of the house can be seen in the gardens. In the 1930s the estate was acquired by Carmarthenshire County Council and eventually converted into the National Botanic Garden for the Millennium.

The Gardens have developed and matured over the years since their opening with features such as the double walled garden and the stunning Great Glasshouse, the largest single span glasshouse in the world designed by Norman Foster and Partners.

Paxton's Tower is now a National Trust property and open year round, free of charge. It offers superb views over the Towy valley. The ground floor is where the carriages drew up and diners emerged under cover to climb to the first and second floors.

In the early years of the 19th century, a spring in Middleton Park was regarded as a spa. Thomas Rees in his 1815 South Wales edition of *The Beauties of England and Wales* describes the spring. Tests were carried out on the water by Mr Accum and Drs Saunders and Babington, who asserted that it was "a chalybeate water equal to Tunbridge Water except that it holds in solution a larger degree of iron and is therefore more powerful." Sir William Paxton erected "hot and cold baths with every suitable convenience for valetudinarian visitors". The waters were recommended for "Scrofulous complaints, for scurvy and other cutaneous diseases, for Hypochondria, Epilepsy, Paralytic affections, Consumption, weakness of the digestive organs, and other disorders attended with prostration of strength. Their use is forbidden in all inflammatory disorders, acute Rheumatism, Dropsy, when the strength of the patient is much reduced, and fixed gout." It transpired that the author had been mistaken, as the baths were for the use of the family and consisted of a single bath, but the waters were piped outside the estate walls.

Llanboidy

The village was originally called Nantboidy, or the stream by the byre, but became corrupted to Llanboidy.

Llanboidy today is associated with the cheese that bears its name and is produced by Sue and Huw Jones just outside the village on their farm at Cilowen Uchaf. The village of Llanboidy is an ancient village with its history going back to the Iron Age when it had a timber built fort, the motte of which can still be seen on the right as the village is entered from the south.

The old market hall with the drinking fountain outside is on the left. The fountain is in memory of Walter Rice Howell Powell MP who was responsible for bringing the mains water supply to Llanboidy. Powell inherited the Maesgwynne estate on the death of his father in 1834 at the age of 15 (the house at Maesgwynne has been demolished and the site is now occupied by the Maesgwynne Mansion Holiday Cottages to the east of the village). He was a magistrate, Lord Lieutenant of Carmarthen and, for 50 years, master of foxhounds. He owned a string of racehorses and built a steeplechase course at nearby Cefnbrafle. In the 1860s he turned the failing Carmarthen Steeplechases into the premier racing event in Wales. He built the Maesgwynne Arms Hotel in Llanboidy to accommodate the London journalists who attended the race meetings. The hotel is now derelict and can be seen on the south-eastern edge of the village. Powell was an important local benefactor, building the local school and the market hall for farmers to trade their produce and machinery. He was a leading reformer, establishing the Three Counties Benefit Society which provided its members with income during illness and a pension in old age. He encouraged agricultural shows and the establishment of butter factories, all to promote improvements in agriculture. He had been called home from Christ Church College, Oxford in 1839, at the start of what became known as the Rebecca Riots, when local toll gates were destroyed by farmers. The young Powell sided with the farmers and stopped the re-erection of the toll gates at Llanboidy and Maesgwynne, so preventing the further trouble that was to erupt in other areas of Carmarthenshire and Pembrokeshire over the following four years.

He entered Parliament as a Liberal in 1880 and served as an MP until his death in 1889. There is a funerary monument, *Grief* to Powell in the churchyard by Sir William Goscombe John RA, the celebrated Cardiff born artist who had been apprenticed to Rodin. The church is

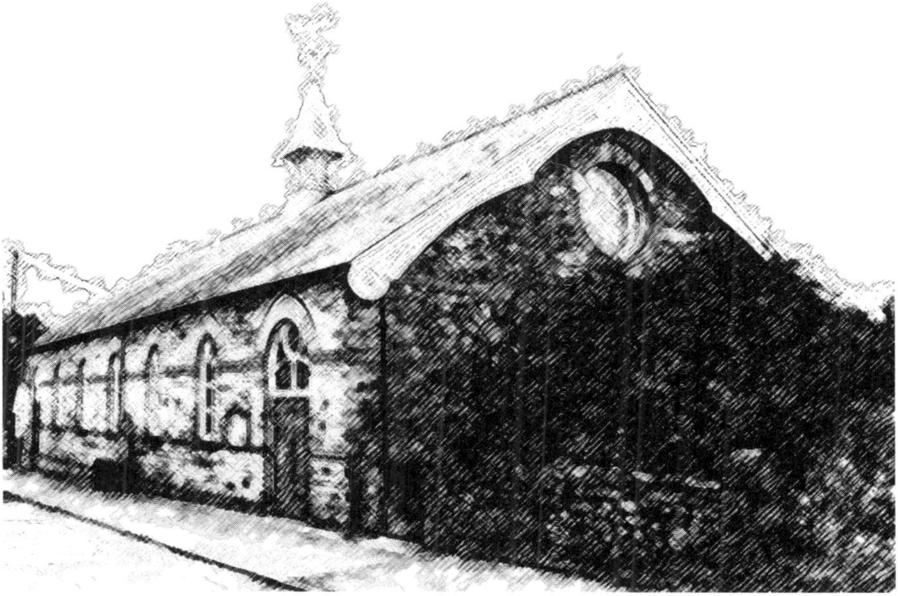

Llanboidy Market Hall

dedicated to St Brynach, a 6th century saint probably of Irish origin, who founded a monastery in Nevern in Pembrokeshire. The church is medieval in origin but was much restored in the 19th century.

To the north of the village is Pemberton's Chocolate Farm.

Llandawke

Llandawke is a tiny parish of just 600 acres one mile north-west of Laugharne. The church of St Odoceus is a redundant church set in a dell. It was taken over by The Friends of Friendless Churches charity with a 999 year lease from 2006. Dating from the 13th century, though probably on a much earlier site, the church is very small and the tower is squat with a pyramid roof. It was remodelled by Sir Guy de Brian, Lord of Laugharne, in the 14th century and renovated in the 19th century. Inside is a 14th century effigy believed to be of Sir Guy's niece, St Margaret Marlos. Originally coloured, it was put in the church in 1902 and has three cracks which some have held represent the belief that her body was cut into three pieces by robbers, though this was

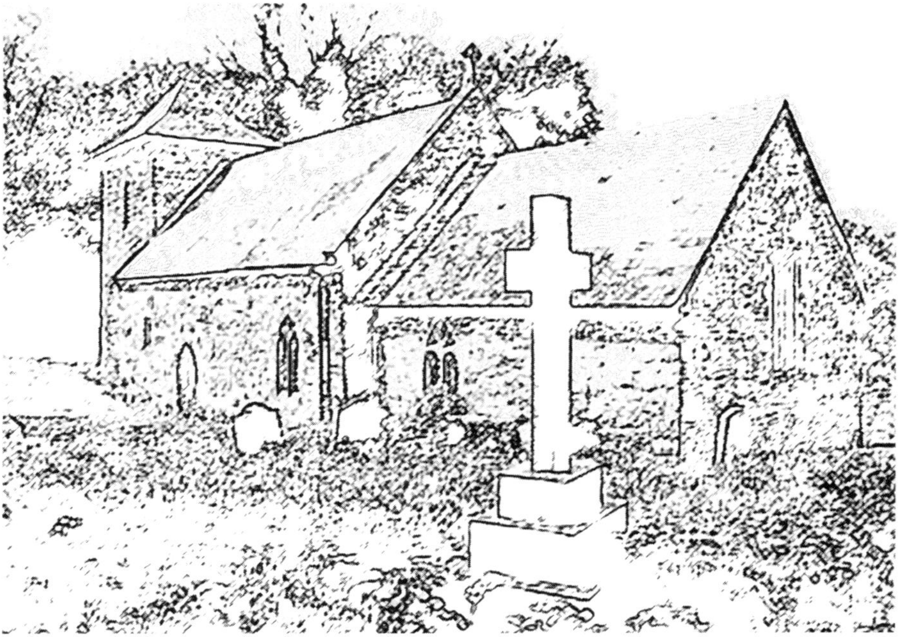

St Margaret's Church, Llandawke

more likely the result of vandalism by Cromwellian troops. A much earlier 5th or 6th century stone slab with Latin and Ogham inscriptions is also to be found in the church. The Latin reads 'Hic Iacet Barrivend filius Vendvbari' – 'Here Lies Barrivend son of Vendvbari'. The condition is poor because it was used as a step at the south door.

The 1882 renovation produced an elaborately carved altar, out of keeping with the simplicity of the church. It was financed in part by a garden fete and bazaar held at Corse house by Mrs Weinholt. According to the *Carmarthen Journal* of 5th May, 1882, Mrs Norton of Laugharne Castle, Mrs Vaughan of Laugharne and Mrs Falkener of Glanymor all had stalls. (Corse House is now the Cors Country House Restaurant in Laugharne with its 2½ acres of landscaped gardens.)

For those interested in epitaphs, there is an interesting moral in one piece of doggerel on the gravestone of Rebecca Uphill who died in childbirth at the age of 25 in 1850:

O ponder well her sudden fall
Ye thoughtless, blooming wenches all

Ye little think who read this stone
How soon the case may be your own.

It is alleged a ghost has been seen leaning on the church gate. She is seen with a broad lilac sash and bow and a straw hat bedecked with lilac ribbons. She was the bride who, along with her husband, was murdered by a jilted lover. Her body was thrown into a pool behind the church while the groom's was found outside the church door.

Llanddarog

Llanddarog today is now doubly by-passed first by the old A48 and by its dual carriageway successor, leaving a small peaceful village with its church of St Twrog and its two pubs. The church was built on the site of a wooden church, in 1854, by the architect R K Penson who was responsible for a number of churches in the county and the exterior of Newton House in Llandeilo.

In the 18th century, Gutto Rowley attempted to rob Lewis a pig drover from Llanddarog on Bristol Bridge. He was recognized by Lewis as the murderer of a tithe collector in Carmarthenshire seven years earlier. He had escaped to Bristol and worked in a sugar factory. He was hanged at Pensarn just outside Carmarthen in 1788. His son met the same fate ten years later.

Llanddeusant

Llanddeusant is a small scattered village on the northern slopes of the Black Mountain. Llanddeusant means church of two saints and the church is dedicated to St Simon and St Jude. The church, with its twin barrel roofs, dates from the 14th century, but legend has it that it was originally built two miles away at Twynllannan and was miraculously moved overnight to its present location. The old Red Lion, next to the church, is now a youth hostel. The view south from the church is spectacular: taking in the two highest points of the Black Mountain, Fan Brycheiniog and Picws Du, nestled below which is Llyn y Fan Fach, from which the Lady of the Lake appeared (see Myddfai).

The village has a Red Kite feeding station, which is well signposted and situated a little over a mile north of the church near the Red Pig Inn (formerly the Cross Inn). Feeding takes place daily, at 2 pm in

Winter and 3 pm in Summer, and fifty or more of these magnificent birds can be seen from purpose built hides.

Llandissilio

Llandissilio is a village which is part in Carmarthenshire, part in Pembrokeshire. The church dedicated to St Tysilio stands in a classic circular llan, indicating its Celtic origins. The church was described in 1833 as having no architectural claims worthy of note.

The village appears to have been of importance in prehistoric times, with a cursus identified by crop marks, dolmens, a standing stone and a stone circle. There is also an iron age fort at Portis Parc.

The centre of the village has a number of attractive older cottages while the outskirts have been developed with newer houses.

Llanddowror

Llanddowror is a village on the road from St Clears to Red Roses. It has a special place in Welsh history because of its rector, Griffith Jones, appointed in 1716. A noted preacher, Jones often held open air services, attracting large congregations but remained committed to the Anglican Church and publicly attacked more outspoken non-conformists. It is, however, as an educationalist that Griffith Jones is best remembered. In 1731 he began his 'circulating schools' whereby a teacher would attend a village and set up a school for three months, often in the church, and then move on leaving a senior pupil to carry on the education. The education consisted of teaching students to read the Bible and Catechism. Over 150,000 people were taught to read as a result of his work.

Llanddowror has another claim to fame. The hill station of Landour in the Indian state of Uttarakhand was named after Llanddowror. The twin towns of Mussoorie-Landour were known as the Queen of the Hills.

The name Llanddowror relates to a legend that a couple in Pembrokeshire in the time of St Teilo had a child each year and then for seven years had none. The following year the wife had septuplets. Realising that they could not afford to feed an extra seven mouths Cynanyw and his wife decided to drown the children. As he was drowning the first child in the River Taf at Rytsinetic, St Teilo happened to pass by and offered to take and care for the children.

The children were raised at Teilo's estate at what was to become Llanddowror. They were educated in the gospels and each evening seven fishes would be found on a rock in the river. When Teilo visited, an eighth, larger fish would be found. The children grew up and left to preach the gospel. They went to Mathry in Pembrokeshire and became known as the Seven Sainted Men of Mathry. The place where they were raised became known as Llanddyfrwyr, 'dyfrwyr' meaning 'men of water', because they were found in and saved from the water and were fed by the water.

Llanddowror was a resting place on the Pilgrims' Way to St David's and in a field behind the church are two stones, marked with crosses, said to mark the graves of pilgrims. The village was also on the drovers' route to London and an unusual feature is the village pound, originally used to store wandering animals but also for keeping animals while their owners were taking refreshment at the Coopers' Arms. The pound was restored in 2000 to mark the millennium.

The church, dedicated to St Cringat has a 16th century tower and 15th century font.

Llandybie

Llandybie is on the road between Llandeilo and Ammanford and named after the church dedicated to St Tybie, a martyred daughter of Brychan, King of Brycheiniog (Brecon).

In 1806, John Rowlands in his *Historical Notes on the Counties of Glamorgan, Carmarthen and Cardigan* wrote: "Llandebie is highly favoured by nature; it is one of the most pleasant villages in the county." The village has expanded dramatically since 1806 but the heart of the village around the church retains its appeal, largely thanks to the building of Gwilym Road in the 1960s which routes through traffic away from the centre.

The River Loughor flows through the village which has a railway station on the Heart of Wales line. The area is rich in limestone and coal deposits and, with the river providing water, was an early centre of industry.

On the outskirts of Llandybie is the Glynhir estate. Today Glynhir Mansion is a hotel. It is Grade II listed. The building was originally a 17th century farmhouse. It was enlarged to form the mansion house of the Powell family before its sale to Peter Du Buisson, in 1770, who enlarged and further extended it during the 19th century.

The Du Buissons were Huguenots who had escaped persecution in France around 1685 but maintained links with family members who had remained in France. While travelling to Ireland in 1770, Peter Du Buisson was delayed by bad weather and decided to explore the area. He was so taken with Glynhir that he bought it at an auction held at the Turnpike House Inn, Llandeilo on the 8th May, 1770 at a price of £33,000.

In the early 19th century, the estate had its own brewery, laundry, slaughter house, smithy, carpenter's shop, mill and dovecote. Peter Du Buisson also set up a knife factory on the estate, between the house and the mill. An example of its output can be seen at the Carmarthen County Museum. Local legend had it that the works were staffed by Frenchmen, though this may have been associated with the rumours that the factory was used to produce arms for the French during the Napoleonic Wars. It is possible that knife production at Glynhir was the result of Du Buisson's friendship with James Henckell who spent some time at Glynhir, dying there in 1823 at the age of 84. The Henckell family were engaged in the iron industry at Wandsworth in London. The Henckells were of Dutch extraction and Caroline Henckell married William Du Buisson, Peter's son.

In 1808 Peter Du Buisson acquired the Llandyfân Forge, four years before his death in 1812.

Richard Fenton on his 1809 tour of Carmarthenshire wrote: "Hence to Clynhir the Seat of Mr. Du Buisson, who came into this country concerned in an Iron Work, which was carried on by the River Lochor, which passes through the farm of Clynhir, now made by great perseverance and profound agricultural knowledge, from cold mountain ground, as good land as any in the County. Here the Gardens, by being well sheltered, are productive of most excellent fruit. To the South of the House, passing the Gardens, you descend into a deep and beautifully wooded Valley, at least a Mile in length, and crossing a wooden bridge over a deep rocky channel, through which the River takes its course, you turn to the left on the other side, and after crossing a little gulley in the Hill, down which a most picturesque torrent constantly pours, as may be seen by the attrition of the rocky channel it frets its way through, you walk down by the margin of the whole river, which, just above you, is precipitated down a steep [sic] high, forming the most graceful and elegant fall I ever saw, with the finest possible accompaniment of Wood."

In 1814 two cousins of the Du Buissons were staying at Glynhir when news came of Napoleon's escape from Elba. They returned to France taking with them two homing pigeons from Glynhir. News of Wellington's victory at Waterloo reached Glynhir by pigeon before anywhere else in Britain. Caroline Du Buisson immediately set out for London on horseback and bought large amounts of Government stock before the news from Waterloo reached London. She succeeded in making a large amount of money that she later used to establish a girls' school locally, finance the building of the church at Llandyfân and refurbish the church at Llandybie. It is believed that the Henckells and Du Buissons were friends of the Rothschilds and that she had travelled to London to inform them. Certainly the Rothschilds had news of the victory at Waterloo before the British Government.

Peter Du Buisson was a magistrate and Receiver General in charge of the taxes for Carmarthenshire, Cardiganshire and Pembrokeshire. His son William was appointed Deputy Lieutenant of Carmarthenshire in 1815 and High Sheriff in 1826. He died, aged 47, in 1828 in Wandsworth. In turn, his son, also William, was High Sheriff in 1870-71. He died in 1894 at the age of 76.

The Du Buissons sold the estate in 1921.

To the north of Llandybie can be seen the considerable remains of the lime kilns, six of which were designed and owned by R K Penson, the architect responsible for the exterior of Newton House in Llandeilo and for designing the nearby church of Llandyfân. The coming of the railway to Llandybie in 1857 encouraged the building of these kilns.

Lime was used as far back as the 12th century for mortar, painting buildings and fertilizing the soil. Lime was also supplied to the steel and chemical industries, but with modern changes in those industries the 19th century kilns could not meet the purity levels required and lime burning ceased in 1973. Quarrying continued until 2002, with limestone and aggregates used for the M4 motorway and other construction. The lime kilns are Grade II listed historic monuments.

St Tybie's church is built on a Celtic llan, though the churchyard has been enlarged. The present church dates from the 13th century and the nave and chancel are slightly out of alignment, an indication of a 'weeping chancel'. The tower was a later addition but still medieval, while a second aisle and lady chapel were also added. In the 19th century, Sir George Gilbert Scott, the architect responsible for the Albert Memorial in London, was employed in the

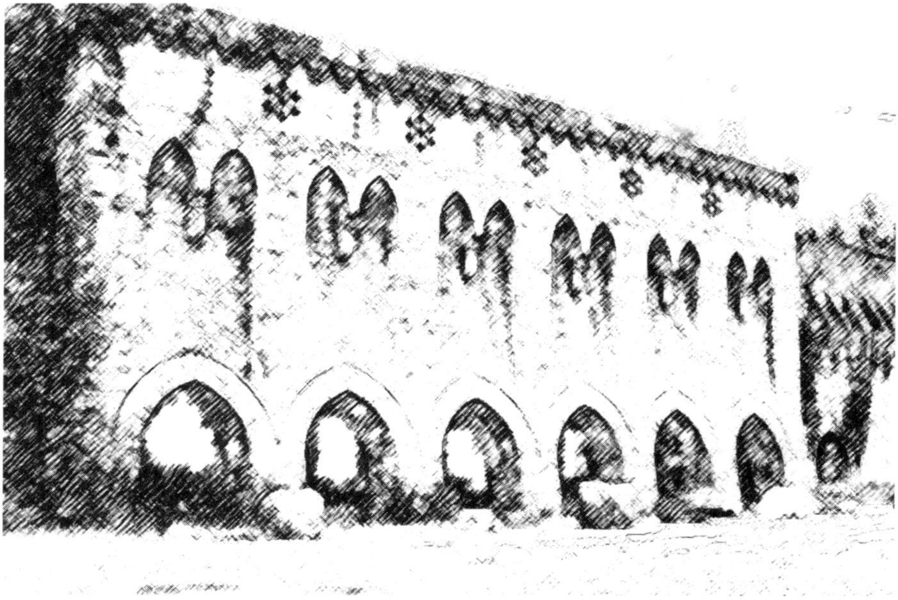

Llandybie Lime Kilns

refurbishment of the church which was largely funded by Mrs Du Buisson. The result has been a rather uniform appearance apart from the chancel where the joinery and monuments are exceptional. The church clock was not added until 1920 as a War Memorial.

Today, Llandybie continues to expand with a number of large houses on relatively small plots.

Llandyfân

Llandyfân today is a scattered community on the western slopes of the Black Mountain but was once a centre of industry and much larger. The name Drefach or little town shown on the Ordnance Survey map gives some idea of the history.

In the grounds of the church is an immersion tank used by the Baptists in the 18th and 19th centuries, but the spring was regarded as having curative properties long before. Known as Ffynnon Gwyddfaen the spring had been regarded as a holy well in the 16th century but its history goes back much further. It was also known as Teilo's Well, St

Teilo having died at Llandeilo in the 6th century, and is shown on some old maps as the Welsh Bath at Llanduvaen. The name Llandyfân denotes the Church of Dyfân, but who Dyfân was is unknown.

Pilgrimages had been banned as an anti-catholic measure in the reign of Elizabeth I. In 1592 a large number of people were apprehended at Ffynnon Gwyddfaen and brought before the magistrate, Morgan Jones of Tregib. He dismissed the charges saying that they were poor sickly persons who had visited the well to bathe in the restorative waters. Morgan Jones was subsequently charged before the Star Chamber in 1594 with failing to prevent pilgrimages.

A chapel of ease had been erected next to the spring and in the 18th century was used by Methodist preachers then by Baptists who used the spring for immersion baptism, followed by Independents. It became known as the Chapel of Mixtures and things deteriorated as the Baptists split into two denominations and the Unitarians also started using the chapel. The situation improved as the congregations built their own chapels and only the Unitarians remained. In 1838 a new minister arrived but was so extreme in his preaching that the church authorities in Llandeilo expelled the Unitarians and the chapel reverted to the Anglicans.

The present church, built in 1864-5, was designed by R K Penson, the architect of Newton House, Llandeilo, the home of the Dinefwr family, and Llandyfeisant church in the grounds of the Dinefwr estate. Penson also designed a battery of lime kilns at Llandybie in an ornate ecclesiastical fashion as well as churches throughout Wales and the Grosvenor Hotel, Chester. The building was funded by Lady Dinefwr and Mrs Du Buisson of Glynhir.

The church has a three sided apse with a south porch. It is built of red sandstone with a stone tiled roof. Of particular interest is the unusual double pyramid spirelet. Inside, the church has whitewashed walls. The three apse, two light windows with a pattern of circles are by Hardmans, the Midlands based stained glass makers who also produced the stained glass for the Houses of Parliament, St Chad 's Cathedral, Birmingham, St Andrew's Cathedral, Sydney and the Chapel of St Andrew's University.

The spring, the source of the River Gwyddfân, was renovated and in 1897 Llandeilo Town was allowed to pipe water from it to the town. Today the steps lead down to the immersion tank but the mechanism to fill it is badly rusted.

The River Loughor passes almost without notice through the village, but once provided the source of power for a number of forges, the remains of which are now overgrown.

Llandyry

Sometimes described as Capel Llandyry, with variations of spelling such as Llandurry, there is a church and a few houses south-east of Kidwelly. The church was classified as a chapel of ease and linked with the parish of Pembrey. It was transferred by John of Gaunt to the Collegiate Church of Leicester in 1353. Of medieval origin, it is built in the cruciform style with a rare 'weeping chancel', where the chancel is out of alignment with the nave. There was a restoration in 1876 when the church was granted a licence for burial, so changing its status from a chapel of ease. The church has been recently renovated and is in good condition.

The farm buildings in the area are mainly 19th century although Moat Farm to the north of the church has buildings dating from the 18th century and the canal over-bridge at Moat is Grade II listed. The embankment of the Kidwelly and Llanelly Canal, later converted to a railway, survives along with the aqueduct built at Moat in 1814-24.

Llandyfaelog

Llandyfaelog is a small attractive village, with a number of older buildings at its centre, just off the Carmarthen to Kidwelly road.

Samuel Lewis in *A Topographical Dictionary of Wales*, 1844, says: "This parish is situated on the navigable river Towy, by which it is bounded on the west; and contains a large tract of fertile land, the whole, with a very trifling exception, is inclosed and in a good state of cultivation. The surrounding scenery is richly varied, and that portion of the parish situated between the turnpike-road from Carmarthen to Kidwelly, which passes close to the village, and the river Towy, is not inferior, for the variety and beauty of its scenery, to any district in this part of the principality... There is an ancient weir for taking salmon and sewin, attached to the Plâs Gwyn estate."

The village takes its name from St Maelog, a 6th century priest, the son of a Romano British chieftain from the Strathclyde area who founded a number of churches in Wales, Cornwall and Brittany. There are a number of villages named after his churches in Wales with variations in the spelling, for example Llanfaelog and Llandefaelog. The church in Llandyfaelog is situated in the traditional circular llan of Celtic churches, though the present building dates from the 14th century. At the time of the Norman invasion there was a monastery of some importance here and, in 1139, the Normans transferred ownership to Ewenny Priory. Later, in 1364, John of Gaunt (Duke of Lancaster) transferred the ownership to the Collegiate Church of Leicester. The church was refurbished in the 19th century and a stained glass window depicts St Maelog.

Among the memorials in the church is one to Peter Williams (1722-1796), ordained as an Anglican but with non-conformist views. He is chiefly remembered for publishing an annotated version of the Bible in Welsh in fifteen parts over four years at a price of one shilling each. In his lifetime more than eighteen thousand copies of his Bible were sold. It was the first Welsh Bible to be written and printed in Wales and did much to preserve the language. While Williams was a non-conformist, he did not want to break with the Established Church and insisted that his two sons were ordained. One son, Eliezer, became vicar of Lampeter and established a school there and was in part responsible for the establishment of St David's College Lampeter, Wales' first university.

The village has an inn, the Red Lion. Opposite the church is a converted coach house, the loft of which once served as the village school.

Llanedi

Llanedi is a small village on the old Swansea to Llandeilo Turnpike, though its origins are much older. There is a pre-historic standing stone, the Bryn-Rhyd stone, standing at eight foot in a field of orchids to the north of the village at Bryn y Rhyd Farm. The church of St Edith from which the village gets its name "is pleasantly situated on an elevated hill, overlooking the Loughor, and commanding an extensive view of great variety and beauty; it has recently been repaired, and enlarged by a gallery." (*A Topographical Dictionary of Wales* (S Lewis, 1844)) Rebuilt in 1861, architecturally it is in a transitional style from Early English to Decorated and consists of nave and chancel, with vestry and tower. The circular churchyard or llan suggests Celtic origins. Parish records go back to 1689. The church is some quarter of a mile to the south-east of the main village which has a popular pub, Tavern y Deri (the Oak Tree Tavern). New housing dominates Llanedi today and there is little to suggest the mining of anthracite that took place in the 19th and early 20th centuries or the importance of the parish. The western side of the nearby town of Pontardulais was originally known as Pontardulais Llanedi.

Records show there was an attempt at education as early as 1703 in Llanedi, when the church warden reported that "We have had lately a young man that taught a few children, but his encouragement being small he desisted some time since." Further efforts at education were made in 1740 when a school was established by Gryffydd Jones Llanddowror. As was the practice, the school was maintained for three months and then carried on under a senior pupil.

In 1613 The Reverend Rhys Prichard was instituted rector of Llanedi, while retaining his Llandovery parish. Prichard is better known as 'the Vicar of Llandovery' and author of *The Welshman's Candle*. His benefice as a clergyman was in the gift of the crown and Prichard received a special dispensation from the Archbishop to hold this living, qualifying by becoming chaplain to the earl of Essex.

George Borrow in his book *Wild Wales* relates the story of the young Prichard:

"Rees Pritchard was born at Llandovery, about the year 1575, of respectable parents. He received the rudiments of a classical education at the school of the place, and at the age of eighteen was sent to Oxford, being intended for the clerical profession. At Oxford he did not distinguish himself in an advantageous manner, being more remarkable for dissipation and riot than application in the pursuit of learning. Returning to Wales, he was admitted into the ministry, and after the lapse of a few years was appointed vicar of Llandovery. His conduct for a considerable time was not only unbecoming a clergyman, but a human being in any sphere. Drunkenness was very prevalent in the age in which he lived, but Rees Pritchard was so inordinately addicted to that vice that the very worst of his parishioners were scandalized, and said: "Bad as we may be we are not half so bad as the parson".

He was in the habit of spending the greater part of his time in the public-house, from which he was generally trundled home in a wheel-barrow in a state of utter insensibility. God, however, who is aware of what every man is capable of, had reserved Rees Pritchard for great and noble things, and brought about his conversion in a very remarkable manner.

The people of the tavern which Rees Pritchard frequented had a large he-goat, which went in and out and mingled with the guests. One day Rees in the midst of his orgies called the goat to him and offered it some ale; the creature, far from refusing it, drank greedily, and soon becoming intoxicated, fell down upon the floor, where it lay quivering, to the great delight of Rees Pritchard, who made its drunkenness a subject of jest to his boon companions, who, however, said nothing, being struck with horror at such conduct in a person who was placed among them to be a pattern and example. Before night, however, Pritchard became himself intoxicated, and was trundled to the vicarage in the usual manner. During the whole of the next day he was very ill and kept at home, but on the following one he again repaired to the public-house, sat down and called for his pipe and tankard. The goat was now perfectly recovered, and was standing nigh. No sooner was the tankard brought than Rees taking hold of it held it to the goat's mouth. The creature, however, turned away its head in disgust, and hurried out of the room. This circumstance produced an instantaneous effect upon Rees Pritchard. "My God!" said he to himself, "is this poor dumb creature wiser than I? Yes, surely; it has been drunk, but having once experienced the wretched consequences of drunkenness, it refuses to be drunk again. How different is its conduct to mine! I, after having experienced a hundred times the filthiness and misery of drunkenness, have still persisted in debasing myself below the condition of a beast. Oh, if I persist in this conduct what have I to expect but wretchedness and contempt in this world and eternal perdition in the next? But, thank God, it is not yet too late to amend; I am still alive – I will become a new man – the goat has taught me a lesson." Smashing his pipe he left his tankard untasted on the table, went home, and became an altered man.

Different as an angel of light is from the fiend of the pit was Rees Pritchard at that moment from what he had been in former days. For upwards of thirty years he preached the Gospel as it had never been preached before in the Welsh tongue since the time of Saint Paul, supposing the beautiful legend to be true which tells us that Saint Paul in his wanderings found his way to Britain and preached to the inhabitants the inestimable efficacy of Christ's bloodshedding in the fairest Welsh, having like all the other apostles the miraculous gift of tongues. The good vicar did more. In the short intervals of relaxation which he allowed himself from the labour of the ministry during those years he composed a number of poetical pieces, which after his death were gathered together into a volume and published, under the title of *Canwyll y Cymry*; or, the *Candle of the Welshman.* "This work, which has gone through almost countless editions, is written in two common easy measures, and the language is so plain and simple that it is intelligible to the homeliest hind who speaks the Welsh language."

Llanegwad

The peaceful, ancient village of Llanegwad is situated off the A40 between Llandeilo and Carmarthen. The church of St Egwad has its origins in the 11th century, but was rebuilt in the 19th century, with the addition of a tower and steeple. Unfortunately, the building standards were poor and the tower caused structural damage to the rest of the church, causing temporary closure in 2002. The church is in use again, though the steeple has now been removed and stands forlornly surrounded by weeds to the west of the church. Inside there are a number of 19th century stained glass windows.

Next to the church is a house named Ty Coffi, or Coffee House. The owners were persuaded to open their home to serve coffee to the ladies of the church after service.

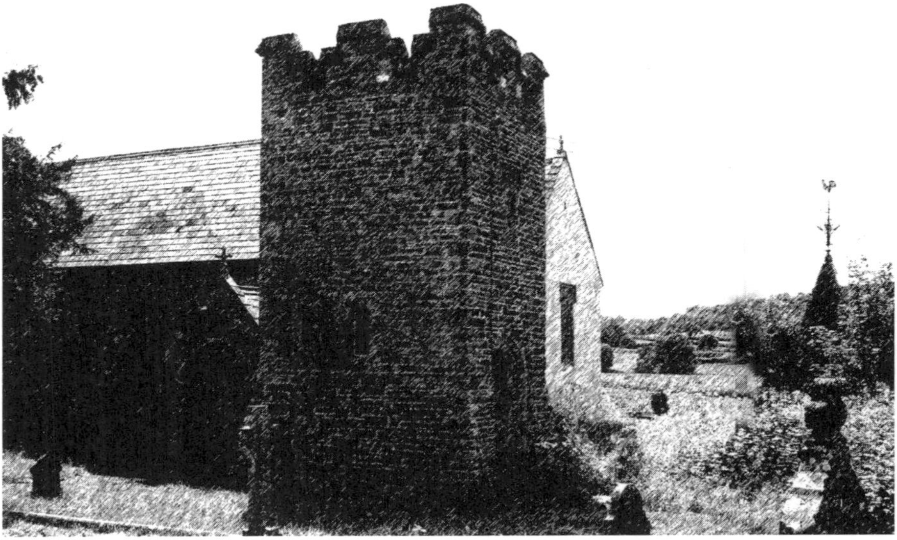

Llanegwad Church with spire in the background

In the Middle Ages Llanegwad was a town or more accurately an ecclesiastical borough with 24 burgesses, 20 burgages, and 60 virgates of burgage land. It grew alongside the monastery that was originally held by Talley Abbey, but passed to St David's in 1239 who then regranted them to Talley at an annual rent of 6 Marks.

Llanegwad Castle came into the possession of Rhys Ieuanc, a son of the Lord Rhys, Prince of Deheubarth, in 1203. It occupied a site to the west of the church known as Pen y Cnap which was the motte of the castle.

Llanfallteg – see Henllanfallteg

Llanfiangel Aberbythych – see Gelli Aur

Llanfihangel Abercywyn (St Michael's at the Mouth of the Cywyn)

The parish of Llanfihangel Abercywyn lay to the south-east of St Clears. The original church of St Michael stood at the confluence of the rivers Cywyn and Taf, but now no road leads to the ruin which is still contained in its tree lined llan. On the opposite bank of the Cywyn are the remains of St Teilo's church at Llandeilo Abercowin, with its nearby Grade II Listed 'Pilgrims' Rest', a 16th century manor house with a vaulted undercroft thought to have originated as a hospital for pilgrims.

The modern church of St Michael stands some way away alongside the A40 dual carriageway together with an unusual Church Room.

Llanfihangel-ar-Arth

Llanfiangel ar Arth is an ancient village in the north of the county centred on the crossroads of the B4336 and B4459. The Church of St Michael stands at the northern end of the village just over 200 yards from the River Teifi. The village takes its name from the Welsh St Mihangel (St Michael the Archangel) and was previously known as Llanfiangel Ioreth. The church is 12th century, with the south nave added in the 15th century. There are some recently added stained glass windows, one of which is by the celebrated 20th century French designer Gabriel Loire and the lych-gate was added in 2003. An indication of the age of the original church on this site can be found in the church vestry. Dating from the 4th or 5th century is a stone dug up from the churchyard bearing the inscription 'HIC JACET ULCAGNIUS FILIUS SENOMACILI' or 'Here lies Ulcagnus son of Senomaglus'. There is also a stone coffin lid or early altar table bearing five inscribed crosses. The church is kept locked, but the key is available from the Eagle Inn opposite. The Celtic Saint Llawddog was known to have been active in this area in the 6th century and it is believed that he set up a monastic community on a spur overlooking the Teifi. The original church was rebuilt in 717. It is likely that the site had pre-Christian significance which is unusual when the dedication is to St Michael.

There was a bridge across the River Teifi as far back as the 13th century and a fine stone bridge crosses the river today. Built around 1850, it has a 72 foot span.

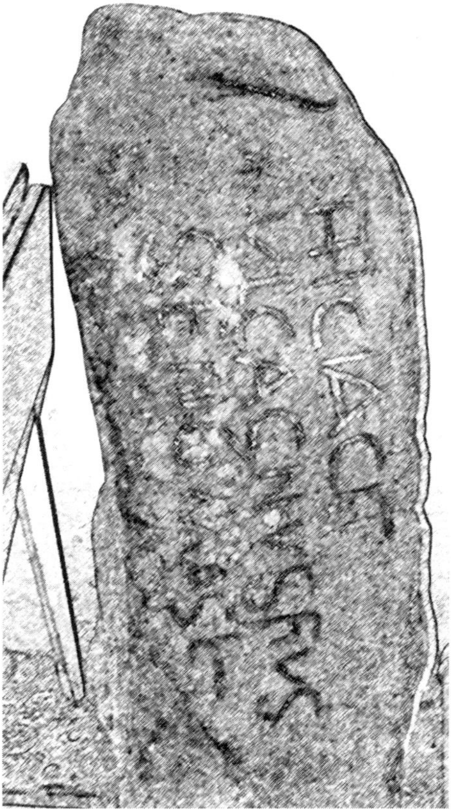
5th century stone, Llanfiangel ar Arth

The village is largely agricultural with a major electrical power distribution depot. To the west of the village is the motte of a motte and bailey castle.

Llanfihangel Rhos y Corn (Church of St Michael of Horn Moor

The parish of Llanfihangel Rhos y Corn lies in the Brechfa Forest. The church of St Michael stands virtually alone in beautiful countryside, with a dilapidated hall alongside, on the road from Gwernogle to

Llidiad-Nenog. The church dates from the 13th century with a second aisle being added around 1500. The earliest church in the parish was a chapel of ease at Gwernogle, just over a mile away from St Michael's to the west. In medieval times St Michael's was a place of pilgrimage. The parish paid part of its tithe to the Priory of St John at Carmarthen.

In 1732, James Thomas, vicar of Llanfihangel, was taken to the Consistory Court of the church by the churchwardens for drunkenness. The Court obviously had little effect and in 1733 the churchwardens engaged Evan Jones, curate of Talley to take services. On Easter Sunday the Reverend Thomas turned up to take the service for the first time in months, no doubt to collect the Easter Offering, and threw the hapless curate out of the church. James Thomas continued as vicar for another nine years.

In 1829 the parish was shocked by the murder of Hannah Davies, a servant girl pregnant by David Evans, a member of a respected local family, who was identified from a boot print left in the mud. Labelled the Cariad Creulon or Cruel Lover, Evans was hanged at Carmarthen but his body was smuggled back to Llanfihangel and buried in the churchyard boundary. His grave is unmarked but can be discovered. In 1878, after 30 years of work, the church renovation was complete and in 1885 Llanfihangel became an independent parish, but after World War I agriculture in the area declined and by 1970 there were just nine communicants.

Llanfynydd

Originally known as Llanegwad Fynydd or St Egwad's of the Mountain to distinguish it from Llanegwad, then an important town, Llanfynydd is a delightful hidden gem of a village, north of the A40, 6 miles from Dryslwyn.

Llanfynydd nestles in the steep valley of the Afon Sannan, a stream where a local itinerant preacher named Jenkins used to pan for gold in the early part of the 20th century.

The church of St John dates from the 13th century, but on an earlier Celtic site, with 16th century additions, renovated in 1861. The windows are typically Elizabethan and there is an unusual gabled extension with a high window on the southern side of the church.

While there has been some development on the outskirts of the village, it retains its essential rural character with its narrow streets,

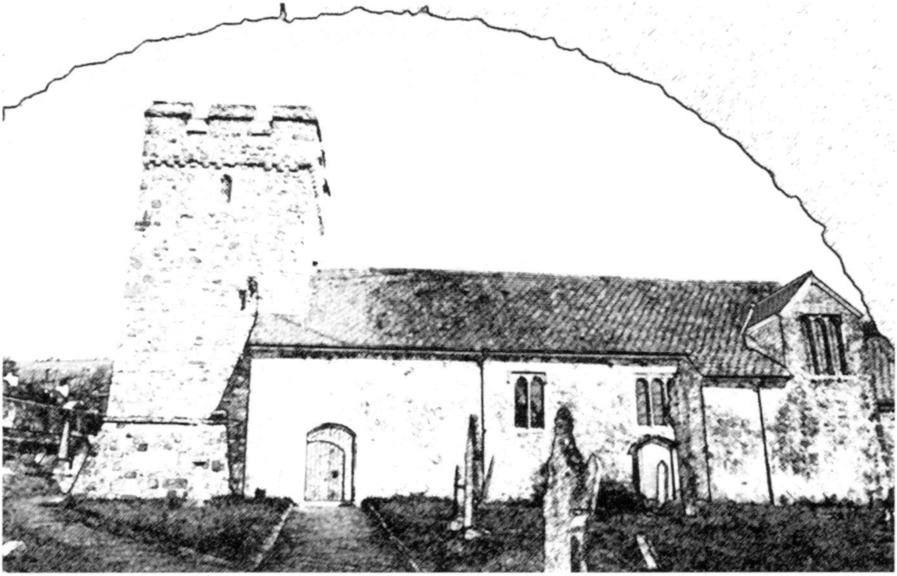

St John's Chuch, Llanfynydd

its chapels and, once, two inns; the Farmers Arms has closed and the Penybont Inn was up for sale at the time of my visit.

The base of a Celtic Cross, the Cross of Eiudon dating from around 900, was found on the edge of the parish. The design was Irish in origin and is now in the National Museum of Wales.

The story was told of a miser and usurer in Llanfynydd who lent some gypsies £300 on the promise of a threefold return. They told him that the money would be left under a standing stone, but that it should not be touched until they were safely back in Egypt. Not waiting, the man tried to retrieve his money but was met with thunder and lightning and when he did manage to start digging, the stone simply sank further into the boggy ground.

In 1876 a Bronze Age burial site was discovered which included a gold amulet with ball ends from the Wicklow Hills in Ireland.

To the north of the village is a Stone Age burial chamber known as Carreg Castell y Gwynt or the Windy Rock, referring to the stone slab covering the burial chamber. To the south-west, overlooking both Llanfynydd and to the west the Cothi valley, is a hill fort Banc y Rhyfel or War Bank.

In 2004 in protest at a proposed wind farm development, the community changed its name to: 'Llanhyfrydawelllehynafolybarcudprindanfygythiadtrienusyllafnauole' or 'a quiet beautiful village, a historic place with rare kite under threat from wretched blades'.

Llangadog

In his book *The Innkeeper's Album*, 1823, William Frederick Deacon wrote:

"Carmarthenshire in particular has solitudes and hamlets of its own, where the inhabitants retain much of the primitive simplicity of their manners. In the village of Llangadock these traces of a better age are as characteristic as the scenery that environs it. ... It provides little or no attraction to the superficial tourist; but stands sweetly, sheltered in the bosom of its own Black Mountains like a pleasant thought in the dreary records of memory. Its neighbourhood is eminently beautiful. A lofty range of hills terminating in the misty peaks of Llynn y Van, forms its barrier on one side; while on the other flows the wizard Towey, bathing the base of a few dwarfish hills, beside which the road winds to Llanwrda."

Llangadog was once a town of some importance, being governed in the middle of the 19th century by a Portreeve and eight burgesses. It takes its name from the Celtic St Cadog, a 6th century descendant of King Brychan of Brycheiniog and founder of the monastery at Llancarfan in Glamorgan. He was a contemporary of St David and has churches dedicated to him in Cornwall, Scotland and Brittany.

There is some dispute as to the dedication of the church which has in many instances been referred to as St David's. In 1282, English soldiers of Edward I are recorded as being "in the church of St David called Llagadanc. They made stables, lodged harlots and took away all the goods of the church and burnt the (priest's) house and wounded the chaplain on the head with a sword by the altar in the church and left him there half alive".

The church underwent a major refurbishment in 1889. Fenton in his *Tours in Wales 1804-13* comments that the building "just by the church", Cwrt y Plas seems to have been a "house of consequence for its day, having wrought stone frames for its windows and door". Fenton was told that it was the former town jail.

Murray in his 1860 *Handbook for Travellers in South Wales and its*

Borders describes Llangadog as "a small decayed town prettily situated".

According to legend, around 400 AD, Marchell, daughter of Tewdric was sent by her father to Ireland to marry Anlach, son of King Coronac, accompanied by three hundred men. The weather was so cold that on the first night 100 men died at Llangadog.

Llangadog Castle or Castell Meurig was a motte and bailey castle and the motte can be clearly seen to the left of the Brynaman road to the south of the village. A modern house has been built in the bailey, but the outline of the horse-shoe earthworks of that part of the castle are visible. It was the subject of a number attacks from 1203 when it was captured 'by catapults and slings' by Prince Maelgwn ap Rhys, changing hands a number of times before being destroyed in 1209.

The entrance to Llangadog from the A40 village is dominated by the Dairy Farmers of Britain Creamery which closed in 2005. The site is now operated by Cambrian Pet Foods.

At the start of the 20th century this was a thriving community with shops and taverns. The names such as Queen's Square are suggestive of a busy centre. Gradually the shops have closed and just two now remain along with a good array of inns. That the village was wealthy can be seen from the large Georgian buildings, which still dominate the centre. There has been a considerable amount of modern development on the outskirts of the village, but the centre retains its character.

A wedding practice common throughout Carmarthenshire was noted in Llangadog. This was the 'biddings', whereby guests were invited to a wedding with a request for a 'bidding' or donation to the wedding couple on the basis that on the donor's own wedding the gift would be returned.

In the 18th century Llangadog was the scene of a notorious murder. On 8th January, 1770, William Powell, Gentleman of Glanareth in the parish of Llangadog, was murdered. Apparently his wife was having an affair with William Williams, a respectable tradesman of Llandovery. Williams recruited eleven accomplices to murder Powell. They arrived at Glanareth by night and forced their way into the house where Powell was drinking with friends and, after a scuffle, Powell was run through. The attackers escaped, but because of snow on the ground they were traced. All but Williams were arrested and removed to Hereford for trial. Two turned King's Evidence and the remaining nine were tried for murder. Six were found guilty and sentenced to death. Two were sentenced to be hanged in chains after death, while the bodies of the other four were delivered to the surgeons for dissection. Williams was captured on a French Privateer in October 1770 and taken as a prisoner of war, only to escape once more.

Llangadog is served by the Heart of Wales Railway and the A40 runs from Llandovery to Carmarthen across the Towy River, while another road follows the River Sawdde before climbing over the Black Mountain to Brynaman.

Llangain

A modern village built around a cross roads on the B4312 Carmarthen to Llansteffan road. The parish church of St Cain stands a little under half a mile to the east of the village, while Smyrna Independent Chapel built in 1834, rebuilt in 1865, and renovated in 1915 is situated on the cross roads.

The present church dates from 1872, "is dedicated to St Synin and occupies the summit of a lofty eminence above the Towy valley" (S Lewis, *A Topographical Dictionary of Wales,* 1844). The first mention of Llangain is in the reign of Henry I, at the start of the 12th century, but Cain was one of the daughters of Brychan, indicating a 6th century origin of the church.

Overlooking the Towy, which was navigable as far as Carmarthen until the middle of the 19th century for ships of up to 200 tons, the parish of Llangain has been occupied since Neolithic times. Myrddin's Quoit to the north of the modern village are the remains of a Neolithic cromlech while Meini Llwydion is another Neolithic cromlech half a mile south-west of the village in a field adjoining the B4312.

North-west of the village are Green Castle Woods with the remains of a motte, known as Old Castle believed to have been built by Alfred, son of Anschetil Driue, who was granted the Lordship of Llangain in the 12th century. The ruins of Green Castle or Castell Moel are on private land. This was a 15th century house, rather than a castle, built for the Rede family.

Tafarn Pantydderwen was a small cottage, which housed the post office and sweet shop, before being converted to the village inn.

The parish proved attractive to a number of wealthy local people who built substantial houses. Fernhill is a manor house built around 1723. It was the subject of the poem *Fernhill* by Dylan Thomas who spent childhood holidays in the house. It was home during the mid 19th century to the County Assistant Hangman, Robert Rickets Evans. Evans never hanged anyone, but legend has it that he imprisoned his heiress daughter in the house in an attempt to prevent her marrying her Hungarian doctor-lover who managed to free her.

Pantyrathno was built by James Richards, who had made his fortune selling milk. It is now the Mansion House Hotel, situated to the south of the village.

Llangathen

The village of Llangathen stands between the A40 and the River Towy in a peaceful spot. The main feature of the village is Aberglasney House, with its gardens. The present house and gardens owe their origins to Bishop Rudd who acquired the estate in 1600 and his elaborate tomb is to be found in the nearby church of St Cathen.

Over the years, the house changed hands and seemed to cause a massive drain on the finances of its owners, with house and gardens falling into disrepair. John Dyer (1699-1757) an artist and poet of some note was the son of Robert Dyer, a Carmarthen lawyer, who purchased Aberglasney in 1710. Among his poems is *The Country Walk* where he describes Aberglasney Gardens:

See below the pleasant Dome,
The Poet's Pride, the Poet's Home,
Which the Sun-Beams shine upon,
To the Even, from the Dawn.
See her Woods and Echo talks,
Her Gardens trim, her Terrace Walks,
Her Wildernesses, fragrant Brakes,
Her gloomy bowers, and shining Lakes.
Keep, ye Gods, this humble seat
For ever pleasant, private, neat.

Major restoration work was carried out on the house and gardens around the millennium and continues with new features being added; such as the Ninfarium (the name is derived from the gardens of Ninfa south of Rome) or indoor garden, opened in 2005, contained within the walls of the house and courtyard and covered with a glass atrium. The Cloister Garden is possibly unique today as it is a survivor of the

Elizabethan style of formal raised terraces that have elsewhere been destroyed by the 18th century landscapers who dictated a more open, parkland view. The pond would have been used for stocking fish for the table. The house was purchased around 1900 by the Mayhew family who were teetotallers and local stories tell of Aberglasney's well stocked wine cellar being emptied into the Pond.

It is claimed that six maids were found dead in their beds in the Blue Room in Aberglasney House, and people claimed a chilling experience on entering this room situated on the first floor of the east wing. There were also tales of lighted candles moving through the corridors. In the 1930s, when the house was unoccupied, Albert Hallet was attempting to remove ivy from the windowsills on the first floor when he saw ladies, dressed in Victorian costumes, peering out at him from the Blue Room.

The church is dedicated to St Cathen, believed to have been King of Dyfed and Brecon in the second half of the 7th century. It has a 13th century tower and there are three medieval family chapels. The 'bedstead' memorial to Bishop Rudd is one of the finest of its type in Wales.

Llangeler

The parish of Llangeler occupies a large area in north-western Carmarthenshire, bordering the River Teifi and taking in the villages of Drefach and Felindre.

The church is dedicated to St Celer, also known as St Gelert. The present church dates from 1858 but occupies a site that is of Celtic origins.

St Celer was a 7th century hermit who lived locally. St Celer's holy well had a chapel and was a centre of pilgrimage because of the well's healing properties. The site of the well is now a Russian Orthodox chapel, Plas Geler, established in 2003 by Priest Monk Vladimir (Lysak). Vladimir is an accomplished iconographer and a number of his works can be seen at the chapel. Plas Geler is a quarter of a mile from the village but by road is slightly further. It is situated on the B4335, a road that offers attractive views as it travels along the Teifi.

The parish hosts the West Wales Museum of Childhood situated on the A484. A privately run museum, it has more than 10,000 exhibits in five galleries.

Llangennech

Llangennech today is a mixture of commuter village and industrial areas. Bridge Street has a number of convenience stores and takeaways. Situated just off the M4, between Pontardulais and Llanelli, on the River Loughor with the River Morlais running through it, the village has a population of over 4,500.

The village name suggests that the church was dedicated to St Cenych, but it is actually dedicated to St Gwynog, a 6th century Celtic Saint. It is believed that a church has occupied the site since 1345, though the present church dates from the early years of the 20th century. The peel of eight bells and the tower were funded by Alderman David Evans of Llangennech Park to celebrate the coronation of Edward VII in 1902.

Llangennech Park was owned by the Stepney family of Llanelly House but early in the 19th century was purchased by the Earl of Warwick and John Vancouver Esq. The Earl of Warwick had purchased the estate from John Symmons. It transpired that the Earl was unable to obtain the necessary capital from his trustees and his friend Vancouver came to his aid. Vancouver acted as estate manager but when he arrived in Wales he discovered that while the survey of minerals had been undertaken, there was no method of transporting them to the shipping on the Burry estuary. The Earl, despite promises of finance, failed to deliver any cash and the venture failed on his death with the Estate reverting to John Symmons. Vancouver had spent over £20,000 on the collieries and other improvements including the planting of 460,000 trees on the estate. Symmons pursued Vancouver even issuing a writ of outlawry and having him proclaimed in the church at Llangennech.* By 1833 the property was the home of Richard Janion Nevill, a leading Llanelli industrialist, banker and magistrate. In the 1890s it was the home of Alfred Sartoris, the husband of Nellie Grant - the daughter of US President Ulysses S Grant. The Park Farm still stands alongside the A4138 but the Park House site is now a housing estate.

Between 1873 and 1931, Llangennech was the site of the Morlais Tinplate Works, situated to the south-west of the village. Coal mining on a small scale had taken place in the area as far back as 1600 when Thomas Lloyd, Gentleman of Llangennech, was recorded as "hath and does coleworks at Llangennech". Several pits were sunk by the Llangennech Coal Company in the period 1825–1874, including the 700ft deep St David's mine at Bryn, which was at the time the deepest in South Wales. The Loughor was navigable at certain tide levels for ships of up to 200 tons and the Coal Company built a quay and deepened the channel. The Company also constructed a two mile rail line and a floating dock at Llanelli, still known as New Dock. Later the Llanelly Railway Company transported the coal, which was deemed by the Royal Navy to be of superior quality. In 1882 the Morlais Colliery sank a slant to two seams. By 1923 there were 569 men employed, though this number fell to 352 by 1945. In 1947 there were two shafts 322 feet deep and 12 feet in diameter. In 1976 a roadway was built under the Loughor to link with the Brynlliw Mine on the Glamorgan side. This formed a single unit with 840 men producing 6,000 tons of coal a week. The Brynlliw shafts were used to extract the coal while the miners descended via the Morlais shaft. The lift was the last in Wales to have a steam powered winder. Morlais closed in 1981. Little evidence remains today of the coal or tinplate industries in the village.

To the north of the village are Troserch Woods, stretching along the Afon Morlais valley. Purchased as a community woodland in 2006, there are the remains of Troserch Mill dating from around 1810. Probably built to take advantage of the high price of corn during the Napoleonic Wars, the mill was reported to be in a state of disrepair by the 1850s though it was occupied as a house until the 1960s. There are also the remnants of small coal mining operations.

* Source *A Memoir Exhibiting the Unmerited Causes of Reprobation and Obloquy which Befel an Unfortunate Individual, Resulting from His Sincere Attachment & Zealous Desire of Improving the Estates and Meliorating the Concerns of the Late Earl of Warwick* by John Vancouver.

Llanglydwen

Llanglydwen is in the parish of Cilymaenllwyd, and is situated to the east of Glandy Cross. The village is set in a rural location with a mixture of old and new housing. There is a village inn, the Penybont Inn known locally as the Bont, but no shop. The church sits on a hill outside the village with views over the River Taf. It is dedicated to St Cledwyn, a son of Brychan Brycheiniog. This is the only church in the country connected to Cledwyn.

The church is 13th century though it was almost certainly built on a Celtic llan, replacing the traditional pre-Norman wooden church. There is a 7th century Celtic cross at the entrance to the churchyard.

The gateway to the lane leading to the church is very grand but was also the entrance to Dolwilym Mansion whose owners, the Protheroe family, were benefactors of the church.

Evan ap Rhydderch originally came from Pencader in the latter part of the 16th century and became known as Evan Prydderch and this became anglicized to Protheroe. The first Dolwilym Mansion was demolished in 1841 and its successor was destroyed by fire in 1908 and rebuilt, although the family never occupied the house after the fire. During World War I it was used to house German prisoners but deteriorated afterwards and was eventually sold by the family in the 1960s. The mansion was demolished in 1986 and the grounds now house holiday cottages.

Llanglydwen had a station on the Whitland to Cardigan Railway, now a two bedroom house not far from the Bont Inn. The track bed was used as a coal bunker, but the platform canopy is still there. Passenger services, which started in 1886, ended in September 1962 with freight services ending a year later.

One and a third miles to the east of the village are the ruins of a medieval chapelry belonging to Henllan Amgoed. Dedicated to St Mary and St Curig, it was rebuilt in 1770 and was still active into the 20th century, but has since been abandoned and sits on private land near Fron Farm. It is clearly visible from the road.

The River Taf flows through the village.

Llangunnor

Llangunnor is a large parish south-east of Carmarthen. The actual village is small, with the church of St Ceinwr sitting amid trees on a hilltop overlooking the River Towy. St Ceinwr was a pupil of St David. The present church dates from the 14th century, but replaced an early Celtic church.

The church contains a memorial to Sir Richard Steele (1672-1729) who retired to his wife Mary's home, Ty Gwyn, below Llangunnor Hill. Steele was born in Ireland and had a brief career in the Life Guards of the Household Cavalry. He founded and wrote extensively for the *Tatler* and *Spectator* magazines (the modern *Tatler* started in 1901, but celebrated its 300th anniversary in 2009, and the modern *Spectator* was founded in 1828) as well as a short lived *Guardian* newspaper together with his schoolboy friend Joseph Addison. With the accession of George I, Steele was knighted and given responsibility for the Theatre Royal, Drury Lane, where he wrote and directed a popular play, *The Conscious Lovers.*

The Dyfed Powys Police Headquarters are situated south of the church.

Login (not to be confused with the village of the same name) has disappeared from the Ordnance Survey map, but the National School established in 1868, and now a private house, is at the junction of Heol Llangynnwr and Heol Login.

Llangyndeyrn / Llangendeirne

Langyndeyrn is an attractive village five miles south-east of Carmarthen in the valley of the Gwendraeth Fach. The church dedicated to St Cyndeyrn occupies a large llan. It was described in 1844 as being "a spacious and plain edifice; and the churchyard is one of the finest and most agreeably situated in the country" (Lewis *A Topographical Dictionary of Wales*). St Cyndeyrn is identified with St Kentigern, the Patron Saint of Glasgow (Scottish St Mungo) but may be another Saint, Kyndeyrn map Kyngar a descendant of Cunedda, an early ruler of the north Wales kingdom of Gwynedd, although there were no records of this saint before 1400. In the renovations of the 19th century nearly 500 skeletal remains were discovered under the church. In *More Mysterious Wales* Chris Barber suggests these were monks who died of Yellow Fever in 547. At the cross roads stands the substantial base of a Celtic cross.

Opposite the church is a circular enclosure possibly used for the storage of wandering farm stock or for the safe keeping of animals while their owners were in church.

Mynydd Llangyndeyrn is rich in prehistoric sites. 'Bwrdd Arthur' and 'Gwal Y Filiast' are Neolithic chamber cairns that may have shared a common covering stone cairn. There is also a 10 foot standing stone from the Bronze Age as well as round barrows, ring cairns and hill forts.

Through the 17th and 18th centuries the parish was dominated by a number of sizeable mansions, but by 1841 these had been deserted by their owners and were in use as farmhouses. William Vaughan, brother of Lord Carbery of Golden Grove, lived at Llangyndeyrn and was responsible for the emigration of a number of Welshmen to the community of Cambriol in Newfoundland in 1617. Concerned at the economic conditions of the poor in Wales, he purchased part of the

Avalon Peninsula. The first settlers arrived in autumn and spent the winter in cabins built by fishermen for summer use. The settlement lasted less than two years.

Vaughan had graduated from Jesus College Oxford and settled in the parish around 1599. In 1608, during a violent storm, the house was struck by lightning which killed his wife.

Llangynin

Llangynin is a village north of St Clears. The church, dedicated to St Cynin dates from the 13th century, with a southern aisle added in the 15th century. It is over a mile from the village on a traditional Celtic llan. St Cynin was a grandson of Brychan. The local river is also called the Cynin. It is thought that Llangynin predates St Clears which was a Norman settlement. The church of St Cynin came under the control of the Priory at St Clears. This was a Cluniac order and was controlled by its parent abbey, St Martin des Champs near Paris. At the time of the Hundred Years War with France this proved difficult and the Priory was dissolved by Henry VI in 1444; its possessions, including Llangynin, passed to All Souls College Oxford.

Llangynog

Llangynog is an ancient parish six miles south-west of Carmarthen. The parish church dedicated to St Cynog, one of the many sons of Brychan, lies three quarters of a mile south of the village. Occupying a near perfect circular Celtic llan, St Cynog's is a low double aisled church without tower. The church was renovated in 1876-78 by the architect George Morgan, better known for his work on non-conformist chapels. The work was paid for by the Morris family of Coomb House.

There were two mansions in Llangynog, Nantyrhebog (Hawksbrook) and Cwm later Coomb House. Nantyrhebog was the older of the two and was owned by the Protheroe family, who were related by marriage to the Vaughans of Golden Grove, from about 1530. Nantyrhebog is now a working farm and the oldest parts appear to be the outbuildings with a 19th century farmhouse.

Coomb House is situated in a pleasant valley (as the original name suggests) to the south of Llangynog. It was built in 1679 by Morgan Davies, a member of a family owning land in Pembrokeshire and

Carmarthenshire. Cwm had previously been a farm owned by the third Earl of Carbery (Lord Vaughan of Golden Grove). In 1805 Morgan Gwynne Davies, heavily in debt, sold the estate to William and Thomas Morris, Carmarthen bankers. Davies moved to Cowin Grove, a property he owned in the north-west of the parish. His son William Gwynne Davies became vicar of Laugharne, Llangathen and St Ishmael's.

David Morris started his bank in 1791 under the name David Morris and Sons but it was later known as the Carmarthen Bank. David died in 1805 and the bank was run by his sons William and Thomas. It was Thomas's son William, MP for Carmarthen and Llanelli Boroughs from 1864 to 1868, who inherited Cwm in 1864. He demolished the neglected mansion and built a much larger mansion in the Victorian Gothic style. William's granddaughter, Lady Kylsant (nee Morris), was the last family owner of the estate which was sold in 1941 following her death in 1937. (Lady Kylsant was the wife of Owen Philipps, MP and shipping magnate and occupant of Plas Llansteffan. Baron Kylsant was jailed for issuing a document with intent to deceive in 1931.). Coomb House was opened as a Cheshire Home in 1961.

To the west of the village lies Twlc y Filiast, the 'kennel of the greyhound bitch' otherwise known as Arthur's Table or Ebenezer, it is a burial chamber consisting of three upright stones and a collapsed capstone situated near a stream that has over the years eroded the mound.

Llanllawddog

Llanllawddog is a rural community adjoining the A485 Carmarthen to Lampeter road eight miles from Carmarthen. The church, a single aisled building, stands on its own. Dedicated to the 6th century St Llawddog, the building is 12th century with major 19th century reconstruction. The church wall incorporates a circular enclosure for animals either to hold animals while their owners were in church or to accommodate stray animals which would be released upon payment of a fine to the church.

Llanllwch

Llanllwch is a quiet village two miles from Carmarthen, lying south of the new cattle market. St Mary's Church was originally a chapel of ease attached to St Peter's in Carmarthen and, in the middle ages, both were attached to the Priory of St John the Evangelist. The parish came into existence in 1857. The oldest part of the church is the tower dating from the 12th century as the body of the church has been rebuilt on a number of occasions. In the early 18th century, the church came under the patronage of John Vaughan of Court Derllys and later of the Edwardes family of Rhyd y Gors. Monuments to members of both families grace the church. In 1872, restoration was funded by the holding of an eisteddfod in Carmarthen market.

Howells in his 1831 book *Cambrian Superstitions* records how one old man who lived near the church swore on oath that he often witnessed spectral funerals and "one evening had the curiosity to notice one, by peeping over the wall. Most of the people in the procession he knew, but perceived some one, whom imagined a stranger, standing apart from the rest, and gazing at them. In a few days after this there was a real funeral, so that he was determined to see whether there would be any similarity between them, and went to the churchyard, but unconsciously stood on the very place where he saw the supposed stranger gazing, which, it appears was no other than his own ghost."

To the west of the village beyond the Carmarthenshire Showground lies Cors Goch, part of a lowland raised mire. It is one of the last six such sites in Wales, with peat as deep as 16 feet giving an environmental history dating back 8,000 years.

Llanllwni

A village on the A485, the parish church is actually at Maesycrugiau, overlooking the Teifi. The church, parts of which date from the 13th century, is dedicated to St Luke, but is likely to have been a rededication from the corrupted name of Llonio Llawhir, a descendant of Emyr Llydaw, Emperor of Brittany and brother-in-law of St Teilo, who is credited with founding the churches at Llandinam and Llanllwni.

Norwood Gardens, a three and a half acre garden, open to the public during the spring and summer, is to be found on the main road through the village.

The village itself stretches along the A485 and parts are separated by farmland. There is a mixture of housing. There is a large timber yard in the village as well as local garages, a church school, the Independent Capel Noni built in 1810 and the Talardd Arms.

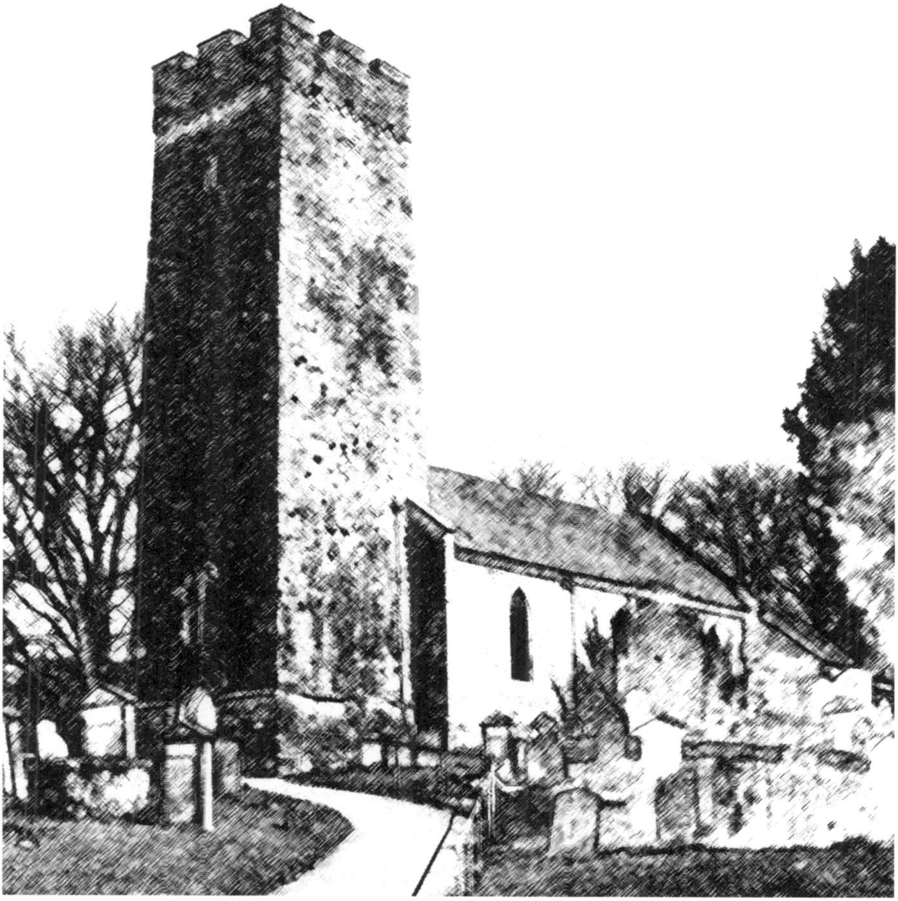

St Luke's church, Llanllwni

Llanmiloe

Llanmiloe lies on the road between Laugharne and Pendine. Today it is typified by extensive caravan parks, stretching along the road to Pendine. The name would indicate the existence of a church, but there is no evidence of this today. To the north of the village are wooded slopes, while to the south is West Marsh and the dunes of Pendine Burrows.

Westmead was owned by Sir John Perrot of Laugharne, but was confiscated by Elizabeth I and gifted to Sir Sackville Crowe by Charles I. He built a mansion and also proceeded to drain the marsh. Westfield Mansion was roofless by 1868 and its site is now marked by Westmead Farm.

Llanmiloe House is set back against the hill. The original house was built by the Mortimers, the Earls of March, but was demolished and rebuilt in 1720 and again in the mid 19th century. During World War II it was used as part of the defence research establishment, which still exists to the east of the village. Planning permission has been given to convert the house into a country house hotel.

Llannon

Situated on the A476 Llanelli to Cross Hands road where it meets the B4306 Pontardulais to Pontyberem road, Llannon is an expanding village with a considerable amount of new housing.

The church dedicated to St Non, the mother of St David, dates from the 13th century but was substantially remodelled in 1841 by Edward Haycock. Haycock, based in Shrewsbury, was responsible for a considerable amount of work in South Wales, including the Cawdor Hotel in Llandeilo and the completion stages of the bridge there and the redesign of Margam Abbey. St Non's was converted from being a double aisled and roofed church to having a single roof over a wide box-like interior.

The village has two pubs, the Red Lion and the Greyhound with the latter now housing the village shop.

There is a horse trough, erected in 1883, on the west side of the main road one mile south of the centre of Llannon. It is fed by Ffynnon Diolch I Ddiw, a holy well that was used for the washing of coins in times of smallpox.

Llanpumsaint

Llanpumsaint, the church of the five saints Gwyn, Gwynno, Gwynoro, Ceitho and Celynin, the sons of Cynyr Barbtruc and descendants of Cunedda. The brothers established the church in the 6th century. There is a stone with Ogham script dating from the 6th century in the churchyard. The church was renovated in 1882 and enlarged in 1933. Next to the church is Bethel Presbyterian Chapel established in 1796.

The village is dissected by the track of the old Carmarthen to Cardigan railway and the Railway Hotel stands near the site of the old station.

Just over a mile and a half north of the village is Skanda Vale, a Hindu temple and monastery. It was established, in 1973, by Guru Sri Subramanium when he moved his small multi-faith temple from London. Skanda Vale now occupies 115 acres. There are three temples: the Murugan Temple, the Maha Shakti Temple and the Sri Ranganatha Temple. Hindu, Buddhist and Christian festivals are celebrated and a Christian service is held every Sunday. The community has a range of animals including a temple elephant, Valli who was rescued as an orphan in Sri Lanka. In 2007 there was controversy over the bullock, Shambo, when he was tested for bovine tuberculosis and condemned to death under the rules. This conflicted with the community idea of the sanctity of life and the ensuing court cases hit the headlines around the world.

Strange happenings were recorded near Llanpumsaint when a countryman returning home about dusk met a spectral funeral. This was not just seen by the coachman, as his forehorse was startled at the sight of the funeral procession. About a week later, the funeral of a local farmer passed that way and the coachman, "happening to see it, declared the incorporeal and substantial funerals were precisely alike in every respect". (*Cambrian Superstitions*, Howells 1831)

Two and a half miles north of Llanpumsaint, on the edge of forestry, stands Garreg Hir, a standing stone seven foot in height. It is visible to the west of the Llanpumsaint to Llandysul road.

The area is rich in tumuli and barrows, with Crugiau Fach half a mile south of Garreg Hir, two circular barrows to the west of the road and a tumulus to the east in woodland.

Llansadurnen

An attractive village west of Laugharne, it is situated in an elevated position overlooking Carmarthen Bay with the MOD testing area to the south. Originally a farming community with three farms surrounding the church, Llansadurnen has seen a small amount of modern development.

The village is dominated by the church of St Sadwrnen, a saint otherwise known as St Saturninus. The church was rebuilt in 1859, on a pre-Norman site, and there are traces of its medieval origins. In the vestry is an early Christian pillar inscribed 'TOTAVAL-/FILIUS DOTHO/RANTI'. St Saturninus was Bishop of Toulouse and was martyred on 29th November, 257 by having his feet tied to a wild bull and, as the bull raced through the town, Saturninus' scull was broken and his brains destroyed.

It was apparently the practice in this parish to brew a Whitsun ale which was consumed by churchgoers after church on Whit Sunday, the day ending in a state of intoxication. The services at Whitsun were apparently very well attended.

Llansadwrn

A small village, just west of the A40 between Llandovery and Llandeilo, Llansadwrn was founded by St Sadwrn in the 5th century. The church site is pre-Norman but was originally a chapelry granted to Talley Abbey by Rhys ap Gruffudd in 1176. By 1539 it was regarded as a parish in union with Llanwrda. There was a restoration in 1883, prior to which there was a gallery and the nave contained box pews. There was at one time a north transept that has been removed; while a chapel was a later addition to the south transept. It is believed that the nave and chancel are 13th century, with north and south transepts and porch added in the late 14th century, and the chapel added to the south transept in the early 16th century. Extensive work including an archaeological survey was carried out in 2005 and the church is now lime washed.

An attempt to convert the Sexton Arms to a private dwelling in 2002 was refused planning permission.

In the parish is Abermarlais Park which once had a fortified manor house. It was probably constructed by Ednyfed Fychan, an adviser to Llewellyn the Great, who married a daughter of Rhys ap Gruffydd and became Lord of the Manor of Llansadwrn early in the 13th century. It was the home of Sir Rhys ap Gruffudd, who commanded the Welsh troops at the Battle of Crecy in 1346. Later it was the home of Sir Rhys ap Thomas, a supporter of Henry Tudor. His grandson, another Sir Rhys ap Gruffudd, fell foul of Henry VIII and was executed for treason, his estates being confiscated by the Crown. Following its purchase in 1795, the old house was replaced in 1803 by a new mansion and the estate was 'emparked'. The new owner was Captain, later Admiral, Sir Thomas Foley, who had commanded HMS Goliath at the Battle of the Nile in 1797. In 1801 he was Nelson's

Chief of Staff at the Battle of Copenhagen to whom Nelson said: "You know, Foley, I only have one eye – I have the right to be blind sometimes" and then holding his telescope to his blind eye said "I really do not see the signal!" Foley became Commander in Chief, Portsmouth where he died in 1833.

Llansaint

This picturesque hilltop village between Kidwelly and Ferryside is dominated by the church of All Saints. It is believed that the old English name of Halkenchurch (Halgen meant saints) was used and shortened to Hawton before the Welsh Llansaint became the norm. The lime washed tower was used as a beacon for shipping it was added to the earlier church in the 15th century. A substantial renovation took place in 1860-62 when the north transept and south vestry were added, giving the church its cruciform shape. The entrance through the tower, which had been walled up, was reopened and a new arch between nave and chancel erected. The walls, other than the tower, were so dilapidated that most were rebuilt and larger windows installed. The church bell was taken from Capel Llangynheiddon at Ferryside when a new church was built at Llansaint in 1875.

There are two stones built into the church walls at Llansaint with Latin text, one upside down. The one inscribed 'VENNISETLI FILIVS ERCAGNI' appears to have Ogham Script, while the other is inscribed 'CIMESETLI AVICATI'.

There was a holy well attached to the church, Ffynnon Saint. After a young girl fell in and drowned, it was covered over and the parish pump placed on top, so the knowledge of its original status has been largely lost.

The road from Llansaint to Kidwelly was known as 'Le Portway' while the main Kidwelly to Ferryside road which by-passes the village was known as 'Ferry-Way'.

Llansaint's most famous son is Gerald Davies the Wales and Lions rugby player.

Llansawel

Llansawel is a small peaceful village in the Cothi valley. Standing on a cross roads it was an important market for the sale of sheep and cattle before their departure along the drove roads to England. A twin arch bridge over the River Marlais dates from 1820.

The church is dedicated to St Sawyl though there is some doubt as to which St Sawyl. Some believe it was Sawyl Velyn, son of Bledri Hir, son of Meyrig, King of Dyfed, who according to Iolo Morgannwg was one of the four kings who bore the Golden Sword before the 'Emperor Arthur'. As a saint, Sawyl is more usually linked to Bangor Isycoed in North Wales. Others take the view it was Sawyl Bennchel, a pagan and ruffian, who converted late in life and founded Llansawel. With the site dating back to the 6th century, the church occupies a circular llan, though burials appear to have been in an area outside the circle. The church is medieval with a squat unbattlemented tower. It was refurbished in 1886 when the roof was heightened and the chancel arch installed. There are four 14th century lancet windows. The

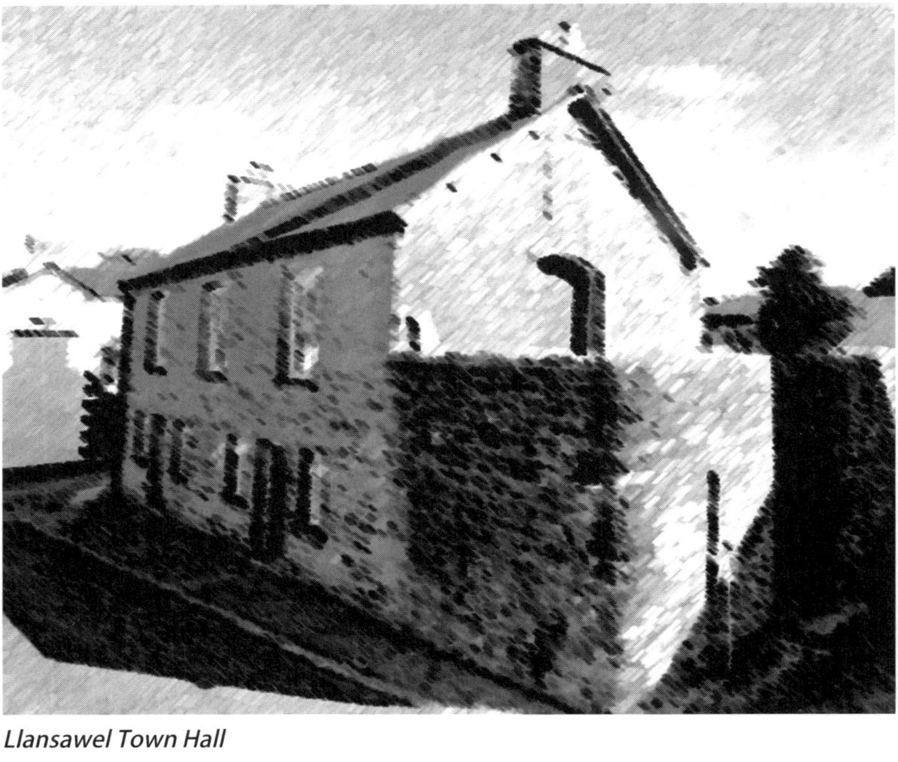

Llansawel Town Hall

reredos is from 1890 and was a memorial to Sir James and Lady Williams-Drummond of Edwinsford.

Sir James sat as magistrate in the Petty Sessions held in Llansawel Town Hall. The former town hall is unusual in that the hall was on the first floor while two double fronted cottages occupied the ground floor.

In the 14th century there was a chapel of Fistyllsawl over a spring just to the west of the village, regarded as a Holy Well. The spring later provided the village with water.

Jesus College, Oxford was founded in 1571 to extend the virtues of learning to the natives of Wales. Between 1602 and 1613 the Principal was John Williams D D, a native of Llansawel, and he was succeeded by Griffith Powell (1613-1620) also of Llansawel, a quite remarkable tribute to such a small village.

Llansteffan

Llansteffan is a seaside village on the western bank of the estuary of the River Towy, south of Carmarthen. It has a fine sandy beach, and is extended except at high tide by Scott's Bay. Some believe the church was established in the 6th century by St Ystyffan, to whom it is now dedicated. It is more likely its origins are Norman and that it was dedicated to St Stephen who the Normans confused with St Ystyffan, a pupil of St Teilo. The church is 13th century in origin, whitewashed except for the tower. It is a Grade II listed building and, unusually, various repairs were undertaken throughout the Victorian period without a full restoration; as a result it retains much of its medieval character. There is a side chapel which belonged to the Lloyd family of Plas Llansteffan and Laques (See Llanybri) and a modern window designed by local artist John Petts. In addition there are traces of wall paintings.

While the village held a market and two fairs, it was never granted a charter. It was, however, regarded as a port, trading with France and Spain until the 17th century. Its ferry link with Ferryside meant that many passed through the village en route to Ireland or on a pilgrimage to St David's Cathedral.

The village is in two parts. Along the beach is a mixture of 19th and 20th century houses opposite the green. Inland is the older village with its High Street, church, chapels and inns.

Dominating the skyline of Llansteffan is Llansteffan Castle, a view painted by J W M Turner. There was an Iron Age fort on the site and

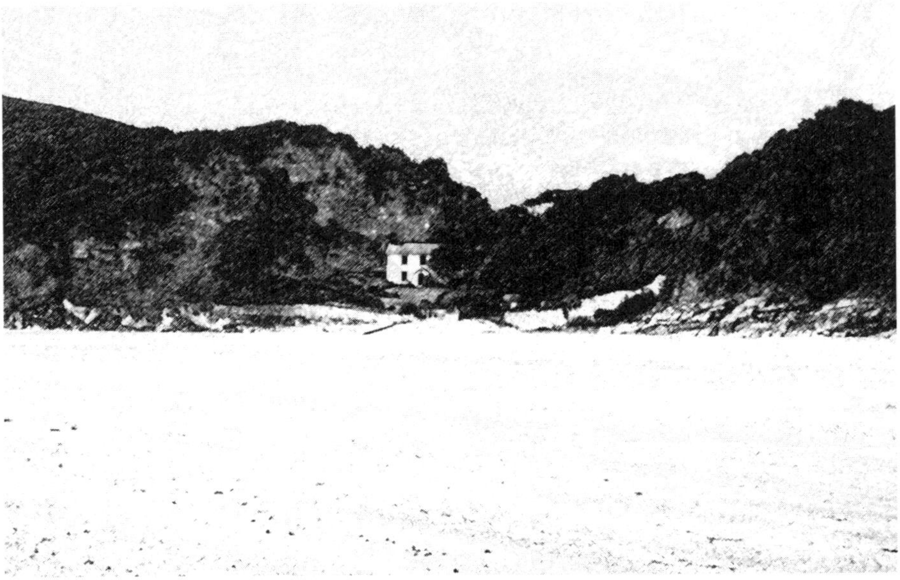

Scott's Bay, Llansteffan

earthworks can be seen to the west of the castle. The castle is in the hands of Cadw and there is no entry charge.

The castle, like most in the area, was taken and retaken in turn by the Welsh and Normans. In 1189 it fell to Lord Rhys of Deheubarth, but subsequently was regained by Henry II who passed it to the de Camville family. A stone castle was then built but the castle was again taken by the Welsh in 1215 and 1257 but returned to the de Camvilles. After Llewelyn the Last's attack in 1257 there was extensive reconstruction and the Great Gatehouse dates from this time. Llansteffan was again taken by Owain Glyndwr. By this time the castle was in the hands of the Penrees family, but returned to the crown to be given by Henry VII to Jasper Tewdor in 1495. Jasper carried out extensive work to the Great Gatehouse but then neglected the Castle and it fell into disrepair. Today it offers magnificent views of the estuary and across the bay to the Gower.

Near the castle is Plas Llanstephan, originally built in the 16th century by Maurice Lloyd who was rewarded for his support of Henry VII by being appointed Steward of Llansteffan. The Lloyds occupied the Plas until 1767 when it was acquired by the Meares who rebuilt the house in 1788. The architect of the stable block was John Nash who went on to design much of Regency London. The house was subsequently occupied by Sir James Hamilton, 1st Marquess of Abercorn, Sir John Williams and Sir Owen Cosby-Philipps, 1st Baron Kylsant. Nelson and Lady Hamilton stayed with Sir James Hamilton at the Plas. Sir John Williams was surgeon to Queen Victoria and, according to Wynford Vaughan Thomas, a descendant of the Physicians of Myddfai. He collected a large library which was donated to the National Library of Wales. In recent years one of his great nephews has claimed that he was in fact Jack the Ripper. Cosby-Philipps was a shipping magnate, starting with one ship in 1888 he eventually owned or controlled a number of shipping lines including the Royal Mail Steam Packet Company, the Union-Castle Line and the Pacific Steam Navigation Company, culminating in the purchase of the White Star Line in 1927. He was at various times MP for Pembroke and Haverfordwest and for Chester. He was made First Baron Kylsant in 1923. Known as an autocrat, in 1931 he was charged with making false statements with regard to the companies' accounts for 1926 and 1927 contrary to section 84 of the Larceny Act 1861. He was sentenced to a year in prison which he spent in Wormwood Scrubs where he was allowed to have outside caterers supply his food. He lost all his honours.

Beyond the headland below the castle is Scott's Bay, named after Captain John Scott who lived in St Anthony's Cottage from 1862. A path leads inland from the beach and behind a door, in what appears to be a garden wall, is St Anthony's Well. St Anthony of Egypt (251-356) was a Christian hermit who had a profound affect on Christianity in South Wales. A local hermit Antwn, following St Anthony's example, lived near this spot. The well water was supposed to have healing properties. St Anthony's Cottage overlooking the bay enjoys one of the most beautiful locations in South Wales. Beyond the cottage is a pathway through the National Trust owned headland of Wharley Point giving extensive views across Carmarthen Bay.

Llanwinio

Llanwinio is a small village in north-west Carmarthenshire on high ground between the valleys of the Afon Sien and Afon Cynin. The church of St Gwynio is situated in an agricultural area on a minor road east of Llanboidy. The present church dates from 1844 but is built on a classic Celtic llan. While digging the foundations of the church a stone was found bearing the inscription 'Bivadus, son of Bodibeva' in Ogham text, dating it to the 5th or 6th century. The stone is now in the Carmarthenshire County Museum. St Gwynio was a 6th century saint and founded the church. He also established a chapel at Cilsant (Saint's Retreat) one and a half miles to the south of Llanwinio. Legend has it that while walking from Cilsant to Llanwinio St Gwynio was attacked and beheaded by Irish brigands and a spring emerged from where his head fell. It is believed that Ffynnon Felen, halfway between Cilsant and Llanwinio, is the spring referred to in the legend

Cilsant by the 12th century was a fortified dwelling, home to one of the oldest Welsh families. The first recorded Lord of Cilsant was Lwch Llawen Fawr. Aron ap Rhys, Knight of The Sepulchre and Lord of Cilsant, went to the Crusades with Richard the Lionheart. Seven generations later, Thomas ap Philip adopted the anglicized form of Sir Thomas Philipps and was an esquire to Henry VII; he married Jane Dwnn, the daughter and heiress of Harri Dwnn, Lord of Picton. Through marriages the various branches of the family became wealthy landowners in Carmarthenshire and Pembrokeshire and Richard Bulkeley Philipps Grant was created Baron Milford of Picton Castle in 1847. A few stones mark the foundation of the old fortified mansion near the farm which stands on the site today.

To the north of Llanwinio are three hill forts: Castell Mawr, Castell Fach and Pencastell. Castell Fawr and Castell Fach were medieval motte and bailey castles while Pencastell was Iron Age or earlier.

Llanwrda

Llanwrda is a village at the junction of the A40 and A482. The church is dedicated to St Cwrda, sometimes known as Cawrdaf. The village was known for the production of rough woollen cloth. According to legend it is the burial place of Owain Glyndwr, leader of the early 15th century rebellion to establish an independent Wales.

Llanwrda was the birthplace of Sir John Powell, a prominent 17th century judge. In 1686 he was appointed a judge at the Court of Common Pleas and a year later to the Court of the King's Bench. In 1688 he presided over the trial of the seven Church of England bishops who had challenged the orders of James II to read the Declaration of Indulgence. They were charged with seditious libel in June 1688 and found not guilty. King James was dethroned in the Glorious Revolution later that year.

In his 1823 parody, *The Innkeeper's Album*, William Frederick Deacon claims there was an inn in the village, The Nanny Goat and Nine Pins with its landlord Mr Zachary Odzooks. Deacon adopted the persona of the village school master, charging one guinea a quarter to "perfect boys in book-keeping, arithmetic and all polite accomplishments. Each young gentleman is expected to bring a knife and fork and at least two shirts. No vacations allowed."

A school had been provided under the terms of the will of Miss Letitia Cornwallis of nearby Abermarlais and the teacher, in 1795, was paid £100 a year, so no fees would have been paid by pupils.

Llanybri

Llanybri is a pretty, ancient hilltop village between the estuaries of the Taf and Towy. Unusually, the name Llanybri did not appear until the 18th century. In 14th century documents it was named Morobri, evolving into Morbichurch, and by the 16th century Marbellchurch and also shown on a 16th century map as Llanvaier, Church of St Mary, recognizing the dedication of the chapel. Llanybri is a corruption of Llan y Bre, or Church on the Hill as it appears in *A Visitation of the Archdeaconry of Carmarthen*, 1710.

The village offers views across to Ferryside, Worms Head on the Gower Peninsula, Laugharne, Tenby and Caldey Island, the Preseli Hills and north to Merlin's Hill above Carmarthen.

The village originally had no church, but a chapel of ease attached to the parish of Llansteffan, dedicated to the Blessed Virgin Mary. The rights to six church incomes (impropriations) including the church at Llansteffan had passed to the Percy family, the Earls of Northumberland. In the 17th century, the 10th Earl had alienated the profits from the living of Llansteffan to Henry Champion of the Inner Temple. Services had ceased and the chapel was in disrepair and Champion granted a lease at a rent of ten shillings a year to William Evans for its use as a nonconformist chapel. Despite later efforts to return the chapel to the Established Church, the legal contract between Champion and Evans held. The chapel continued to hold services until 1960 and has since fallen into ruins. A rift among the nonconformists led to Capel Newydd being established in 1813. The Old Chapel is a Grade II listed building on an island of roads in the centre of Llanybri, next to the Farmers Arms. It was referred to as the 'marbell church' and whether it was at one time painted white, giving it the appearance of marble is open to conjecture.

In 1852 Miss Elizabeth Lloyd of Laques Mansion funded the building of Holy Trinity Church on the outskirts of the village. It was consecrated in 1861 and Llanybri was created a parish in its own right until 1957 when it was joined once more with Llansteffan. The church was designed by J L Collard. It has an octagonal tower and contains a set of marble texts.

Laques Mansion was originally built by the Rede (Later Reed) family of Green Castle in Llangain. In 1616 it was purchased by Rees Lloyd the Younger. The Lloyds are one of the oldest families in West Wales, tracing their ancestry back to Uchelwr (Welsh knight) Cadifor ap Dinawal of Castell Hywel. Morris Lloyd had supported Henry VII at the Battle of Bosworth and was rewarded by being appointed as Seneschal of the Lordship of Llansteffan. The main family lived at Plas Llansteffan, but the Laques branch was wealthy in its own right. Miss Elizabeth Lloyd was the last in her line when she died in 1870 and the mansion was let to farming tenants. By 1976 the house was in poor condition but new owners at that time started to refurbish. The house took its name from the stream that runs down the valley to St Anthony's Well.

During the 1940s, Llanybri was the home of husband and wife poets Keidrych Rhys and Lynette Roberts. They lived at Ty Gwyn, a two roomed whitewashed cottage. Dylan Thomas knew them and was best man at their wedding. He was rowed across the estuary from Laugharne to visit. He referred to Keidrych as a 'turnip' who "now has little turnips growing all over his top", no doubt referring to their children, while he noted that Lynette was "A curious girl, a poet, as they say, in her own right with all the symptoms of hysteria." Rhys launched the *Wales* periodical and Roberts wrote *Poem from Llandybri* and her two volumes of verse were published by T S Elliot. A visitor to their home was George Woodcock, the Canadian anarchist and author, who in his autobiography *Letter to the Past* wrote of the primitive farming methods he found locally: "Llanybri was the last place in Britain where I saw a field of barley being cut with sickles. But all these people seemed to get along well and if there were no rich men in Llanybri, there were no paupers either. An independence of mind had sprung from this economic simplicity." Lynette is buried in Llanybri churchyard. Since her death her poems have been re-published and she has gained much greater recognition.

Llanybydder

The derivation of the name Llanybydder is open to conjecture. Llan, refers to church or more properly the area surrounding the church, while 'y bydder' is of the deaf. This may refer to a female religious order founded by Gwenllian of Blaen Tren. The oldest surviving cottage in Llanybydder is Gwrdy Cottage which was originally the hospitality wing of the order. One can surmise that if the women had taken a vow of silence, visitors might believe the women were deaf. Thomas Morgan, in the 1912 edition of his *Place Names of Wales*, said that "some think the right wording is LlanyhyMair, the church of the Ambuscade" but adds that it may be a corruption of Llanbedr (Church of Peter to whom the church is dedicated). In an earlier edition, he suggests it is a corruption of 'Pedry Peter'

Llanybydder is sometimes referred to as a town, but with a population of just over 1,400 it is today a village in the north of Carmarthenshire on the River Teifi, linked with Rhydycymerau administratively as Llanybydder and Rhydycymerau Community Council.

It retains its cattle market, but is probably best known for its horse fairs held on the last Thursday of each month. On fair days the village is packed with people and horses.

There has been a settlement here since before the Romans, with the remains of an Iron Age settlement on the hill overlooking the village. Highmead House, above the village, is now a centre for Muslim studies.

The church of St Peter dates back to the 13th century and has a large tower which is earlier in style to the rest of the church and may be 12th century. The church was attached to Carmarthen Priory.

The Aberystwyth to Carmarthen rail line ran through the centre until 1965 and the station area now provides a large car park. The village is on two distinct levels, the lower part has the church, market and old station and leads on to the bridges over the River Teifi, while the upper part of the village lines the A485 Carmarthen to Lampeter road.

Llanycrwys (Church of the Cross)

Llanycrwys is a parish in the north of the county, separated from the Caio parish by the River Twch. It stretches to the Llanwrda to Lampeter road in the south and the parish of Cwmann to the west, while to the north is the Ceredigion border. In addition to Llanycrwys, the parish includes the hamlet of Ffaldybrenin within its borders.

The Grade II listed church of St David, a farm and one other house stand alone near the village of Ffarmers. The church is a simple single nave with no tower. It was refurbished in 1892. In the corner of the churchyard is an animal pound that would have been used to store stray animals until claimed by their owner who was charged a fine, or if unclaimed the animals would be sold at market. The church was visited by Bishop Baldwin and is mentioned in his itinerary of 1188. Gwynfardd, the 12th century Welsh poet described Llanycrwys as a new monastery, but there is no evidence of this. The area was part of Trefwyddog which, in the mid 9th century, was recorded as a grant to St Teilo's monastery at Llandeilo in the Lichfield Bible. In the 14th century the church, then known as Llanddewicrwys, was confirmed as being attached to Talley Abbey and the monks had a grange in the parish at Mynachty (Monk's House), described as a township, to provide food for the monks. 19th century books describe Mynachty as a hamlet on the Roman Road Sarn Helen, but there is no trace on modern maps.

Marking the boundary between Carmarthenshire and Ceredigion is Hirfaen Gwyddog, a 16 foot standing stone, 1.5 miles north-west of the church. It is situated above the Tristar Horsebox base at Esgairgoch. It has an inscription dating from 1874, but this stone has the first written record of any stone in Wales, having been first mentioned in the 8th century when it was called 'behet hirmain' in the Lichfield Bible. (This bible was written in Llandeilo and given to Lichfield Cathedral. A digital copy is on view at St Teilo's in Llandeilo and it contains the first ever example of written Welsh.) It is also mentioned by Gwynfardd as marking the boundary of Llanddewi Brefi parish.

Llanycrwys was the home of Chwermon Fawr, a legendary giant of Wales who lived at Llwyn Chwermon.

Llidiad Nenog (Stile to the Nenog)

A small community 1,000 feet up on the edge of the Brechfa Forest. There are a number of farms and cottages as well as a small number of modern houses. The Independent Chapel is small and dates from 1869. The Afon Nenog rises just to the west.

Login

Set in the Taf valley, Login is a delightful small village set in a steep valley. Almost certainly developed as a mill village, there was a mill just above the bridge, it is believed that the name derives from the Welsh 'halogyn' meaning a 'dirty stream'.

The old railway, the Whitland and Cardigan line (known as the Cardi Bach), ran through the valley and the route is still visible. Login had its own station opened in 1875 and closed in 1962. The station is now a private house and while the platform is still visible, the track has been filled to platform level.

Carmarthenshire County Council built its first bridge in the village in 1891 and this is celebrated by a plaque on the bridge.

Calvaria Chapel is a Baptist chapel established in 1828 and rebuilt in 1877. There is an immersion pool outside Chapel House.

Outside the village, Cilymaenllwyd Church dedicated to Saints Philip and James is now a private dwelling.

Maenlle-Gwaun (Stony Heath)

Maenlle-Gwaun is an unsignposted hamlet south of Newcastle Emlyn consisting of ribbon development of mainly modern bungalows with older farm buildings. The road runs along a ridge in open countryside towards Drefach-Felindre between the valleys of the Nant Esgair and Nant Bargod. There is a village hall.

Maesybont (The Bridge Field)

Maesybont is a small community on the B4297 between Gorslas and Dryslwyn. It is a ribbon development centred on the bridge, which crosses the Gwendraeth Fach, and the village Primary School. Most of the housing in the centre is older stock, while a small number of modern properties have been built to the north-west to take advantage of the views over the Towy valley. Just outside the village is the 1923 Hebron Evangelical Hall.

Maesycrugiau (The field of the small hillocks)

A beautiful quiet village on the River Teifi with the Llanllwni parish church of St Luke's and the Old Railway Inn near Pontllwni (Llwni bridge). The Teifi passes through a wooded gorge beneath the church and there is a walk into the gorge from the bridge.

Maesycrugiau had its own station on the Lampeter to Carmarthen line. In 1890 it was the scene of an accident when the boiler of the engine *Caermarthen* blew up, sending the dome into the Teifi.

Maesycrugiau Manor was rebuilt in the revivalist style after a fire in 1902. It was the home of the Mansel family. Sir Courtenay Mansel was briefly the Liberal MP for Penryn and Falmouth (1923-1924) but later switched to the Conservative party. Sir Courtenay lost his baronetcy when it was discovered that his grandparents' first marriage in Scotland, which had been thought to be ineffective, was in fact legal and the title belonged to his uncle who had been thought illegitimate. Maesycrugiau came in to the Mansel family in 1878 following the marriage of Sir Richard Mansel, 12th Bart with Maud Margaretta Jones, daughter of John Jones the previous owner. Earlier owners of the estate included the Lloyds and in 1609 Lewys Dwnn stayed as the guest of David Lloyd while he researched the family pedigree. The estate passed to the Thomas family in the 18th century and then to John Jones in 1862. More recently it has been a hotel and country club and was converted back to a private house in 1994. It is now offered for holiday rental.

Three quarters of a mile south-west of the church where Nant Cwm-du joins the Teifi is Castell Pyr, a prehistoric fort with double ramparts and ditches on a hill 100 feet above the river.

Manordeilo (Welsh Name Maenordeilo)

Manordeilo village is medieval in origin, the name coming from the village commote and later hundred of Manor Deilo. Stretching along the A40, which follows the line of the Roman road, much of the village is of modern development. A horde of Bronze Age gold ornaments in the form of cuff-like bracelets were discovered near the road and are now at the National Museum of Wales.

Marros (Great Moorland)

Marros is a small village in the far south-west of Carmarthenshire between Pendine and the Pembrokeshire border. St Lawrence Church is situated just off the cross roads near the unusual War Memorial built in the style of a Neolithic tomb similar to those at Garness Farm. The church is from the 13th-14th century and the dedication to St Lawrence is thought to have been due to Norman influence as there was an earlier Celtic church on this site. St Lawrence was martyred by being roasted on a gridiron by order of the Emperor Valerian and he is depicted in stained glass in the church. On the walls of the churchyard are the carved initials of parishioners responsible for the maintenance of each section of wall.

A little over a mile south-west from the church is an Iron Age hill fort overlooking the sandy beach and the wooded valley of Teague's Wood.

The cliffs above the sandy beach are popular with paragliders and farmers have diversified into the leisure field with clay pigeon shooting and horse riding.

Meidrim

Meidrim is an attractive village west of Carmarthen to the north of St Clears. It stands on a cross roads and a bridge over the Afon Dewi Fawr. The origins of the name are lost in time, but one suggestion is May Ridge, implying high ground used for summer pasture. The Norman church of St David occupies a pre-Roman fortification and, as with many Carmarthenshire churches, lacks a tower.

One native of Meidrim was John Evans, Chaplain to George II and non-resident vicar of Eglwys Cymyn. Like many priests in the county, he was a graduate of Jesus College, Oxford.

The vicar of Meidrim, the Reverend Stephen Hughes, was ejected from the parish in 1660 on the restoration of the monarchy. He continued to preach and teach until his death in 1688. He was responsible for publishing the collected works of Rhys Prichard, vicar of Llandingad in Llandovery (See Llanedi).

According to legend, around 400 AD, Marchell, daughter of Tewdric was sent by her father to Ireland to marry Anlach, son of King Coronac, accompanied by 300 men. The weather was so cold that on the first night 100 men died at Llangadog and on the second night a further 100 died at Meidrim. Marchell and Anlach married and their son was Brychan who became King of Brycheiniog and fathered some 12 to 63 children (depending on which of the Welsh, Cornish, Irish and Breton versions of his life you take), many of whom became saints in Wales, Brittany and Cornwall. This story does however give some idea of the ancient origins of the village.

Meinciau (Bank)

Meinciau is a village at a cross roads on the Pontyates to Carmarthen road. There has been considerable modern development but a community had grown up around the Black Horse Inn and Soar/Moriah Baptist chapel which was first established in 1828.

Apart from farming, there was a considerable amount of quarrying for the millstone grits of Mynydd Llangyndeyrn. The area was fashioned by glacial erosion and at Meinciau Mawr, just west of the cross roads, is a feature known as a roche moutonnee or sheepback. It is a tear-drop shaped hill that tapers in the up-ice direction.

Merthyr

Merthyr is a tiny village three miles west of Carmarthen; the name implies a church sanctified by a saint's bones. It is found down a narrow lane where there is the church of St Martin, prettily situated on a knoll at the head of a narrow dingle. The road beyond the church is signposted as 'Not Suitable for Motors'.

In the parish is Derllys Court, now a golf course, but the Court originated back in the early 16th century. It passed through several families, including the Vaughans of Golden Grove. By 1800 it was in ruins and timbers from the old mansion were used in the building of the substantial farmhouse. The golf clubhouse is to the south of the farm and is accessed from the A40 via the B4298. Also in the parish is Castell Y Gaer, just south of the B4298. Merthyr Fach is a small collection of houses west of Merthyr in the Cywyn valley.

Milo

Milo is a village between Gelli Aur and Llandybie. Old Milo Independent Chapel was built in 1828 and subsequently rebuilt in 1850. New Milo Chapel, a much larger building, was built in 1904 opposite the original chapel, which is still used as a hall and Sunday School. The village primary school, Ysgol Nant Y Groes, is still in use. There is some 19th century or earlier housing but most of the village is modern, taking advantage of this quiet situation near the upper reaches of the Afon Marlais.

Myddfai (May Meadow)

Myddfai is a beautiful village between Llandovery and the Black Mountain. It is now the Welsh home of Prince Charles, who purchased the Llwynywormwood estate in 2007, and was where

Prince William and Kate Middleton spent their immediate post wedding honeymoon.

The village has a long history and is associated with the Physicians of Myddfai and the legend of the Lady of the Lake. According to the story, a young man named Rhiwallon, the son of a widow whose farm was Blaen Sawdde near Llanddeusant, was tending his sheep at Llyn y Fan Fach, a lake beneath Carmarthen Fan, when he saw a beautiful woman. He offered her some bread, but she replied that his bread was too hard and disappeared under the waters of the lake. The lad was infatuated with the woman and returned day after day until she eventually agreed to marry him. She warned that if he struck her three times, however gently, she would leave him. She emerged from the lake with an array of fine cattle and sheep. They lived happily and had three sons. But on three occasions he tapped her shoulder, first because she delayed taking their first son to the christening because it was too hot, second because she cried at a wedding because she knew that the bride would soon die and third when she laughed at the groom's funeral because she knew he was happy to be reunited with his bride. True to her word she returned with her sheep and cattle to the lake. She did however appear to their sons, Cadwgan, Gruffydd, and Einion, at Llidiad y Medygon (The Doctor's Gate) and taught them how to use medicinal herbs. The sons became well known for their expertise and they and their children became known as the Physicians of Myddfai. In the 12th century they served the Lord Rhys, who granted them land at Myddfai. Their line continued to practice locally until the death of John Jones in 1739, though Sir John Williams surgeon to Queen Victoria could trace his ancestry back to the Physicians. John Jones' gravestone is in the church.

The area around Myddfai and Llyn y Fan Fach is still rich in medicinal herbs. The home of one of the Physicians' descendants, Llwyn Meredydd, still in existence, was the site of the herb garden. Wormwood was one of the herbs commonly used and Prince Charles' property Llwynywormwood Farm means Wormwood Grove.

St Michael's church is at the heart of Myddfai. A Grade I listed building, it dates from the 13th century with a second aisle added in the 15th century. Several restorations have taken place over the years and the bellcote was an addition by Penson in 1876.

Recent initiatives have meant a regeneration of life in the village with a new village hall and a social enterprise, Myddfai Trading Company, set up with various crafts and medicinal herb products being produced.

Mynyddygarreg (Stone Mountain)

Mynyddygarreg or Stone Mountain is a village on a ridge between the Gwendraeth Fawr and Gwendraeth Fach valleys near Kidwelly. Its most famous inhabitant was the Welsh and British Lions Rugby player Ray Gravell, who went on to become a radio broadcaster, actor and member of the Gorsedd of Bards. After developing diabetes, he died, in 2007, at the age of 57. A road has been named after him and a statue of him, made from stone cut from the village, has been erected outside the Parc y Scarlets rugby stadium.

To the west of the village is Maes Gwenllian or Gwenllian's Field, the site of a battle in 1136 between the Welsh, under Princess Gwenllian, and the Normans, under Maurice de Londres. Gwenllian was a princess of Gwynedd in North Wales who married Gruffydd ap Rhys, prince of the local kingdom of Deheubarth, whose father had been killed by the Normans at the Battle of Brecon in 1093. A rebellion had started in Breconshire and Gruffydd travelled to North Wales to seek assistance from his father-in-law. Meanwhile Maurice de Londres started to attack the Welsh of Deheubarth and Gwenllian was forced to raise an army to attack Kidwelly. The Welsh were routed and one of Gwenllian's sons was killed in battle while Gwenllian and another son were captured and beheaded. In the months following, Gruffydd avenged his wife's death with significant victories over the Normans before his own death in 1137. Gwenllian was the only British woman other than Boudica to lead an army into battle. Her youngest son, Rhys, re-established the fortunes of the family and ruled Deheubarth.

Between Mynyddygarreg and Kidwelly is the Kidwelly Industrial Museum based in the former tinplate works.

To the south of Mynyddygarreg is Capel Teilo Road. There was once a chapel dedicated to St Teilo but all that remains is a large stone which marks the north-east corner. Below the chapel is Pistyll Teilo, Teilo's Pool. Steps led down to the pool but these have now disappeared and the pool is virtually inaccessible. Tradition has it that the water was finer than wine and had restorative powers for bruises and sprains. It is said that a ghost haunts the pool wailing "It is long and cold and tiresome to wait for the descendants of Wil Wattar". Spirits and corpse candles have been seen on Capel Teilo Road and locals still prefer to avoid this road at night.

Nantgaredig (Gentle Stream)

Nantgaredig is a small village, largely lying between the A40 and the River Towy, that grew with the railway station which served the nearby village of Llanegwad. The line, now dismantled, ran from Carmarthen to Llandeilo and crossed the Cothi and Towy by bridges, south of Llanegwad, that are no longer. There are two small standing stones in a field behind houses in the village indicating an earlier settlement nearby. The goods yard was used by Carmarthen Farmers until 2002 and the old single storey station building has had a first floor added.

South of the village is a three arched bridge over the River Towy. A flood in 1931 washed away part of the bridge leaving only one third intact. A bridge had been built here in 1779 but had collapsed in 1781. Five years later the present bridge known as Pont Llandeilo yr Ynys (sometimes shown as 'Rwnws') was built by the Edwards family of Pontypridd at a cost of £1,200. Unlike the bridges at Dolauhirion (see Cilycwm) and their most famous bridge at Pontypridd, this Edwards' design was not single span, but engineers reported, that

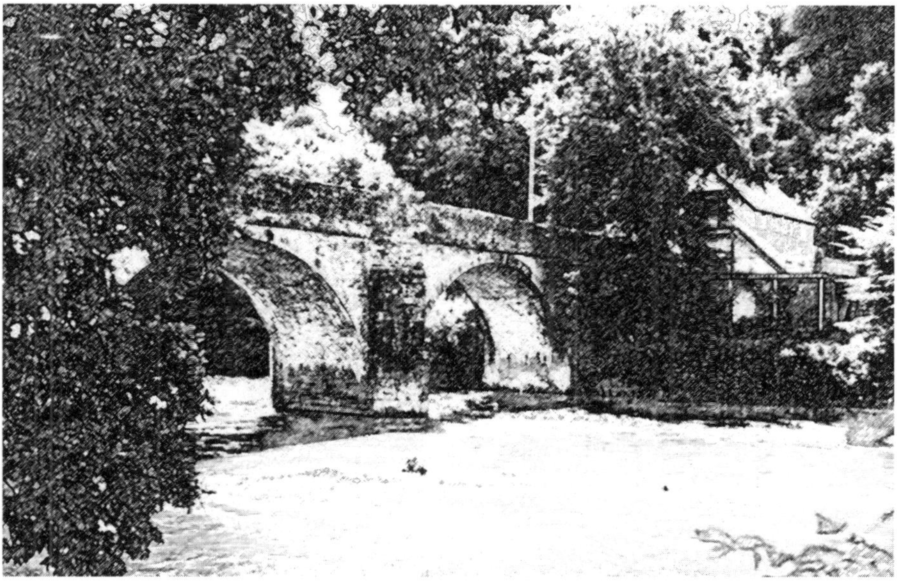

Nantgaredig bridge

after the 1931 disaster, the arches stood firm owing to the excellence of the masonry. Repairs in 1931 cost £6,000. The bridge is Grade II listed.

The bridge was erected by the Llandilo Rwnws Turnpike Trust to enable farmers north of the Towy access to the limestone at Llanddarog. On 7th July, 1843 the toll gate was destroyed by a hundred Rebecca Rioters and the special constable guarding the bridge was horsewhipped. The bridge has seen a number of famous characters over the years. United States President Jimmy Carter fished here and, during World War II, the Home Guard assaulted the celebrated Austrian Philosopher, Ludwig Wittgenstein, as he crossed the bridge, because of his suspicious German accent.

Just west of the bridge is the pumping station used to extract water from the River Towy. 55 million gallons a day are pumped through a 66 inch diameter main to the Lliw reservoirs south of Ammanford and from there, via the Felindre water treatment works, water is supplied to a wide area of South Wales as far as the outskirts of Cardiff. When the normal river flow drops below 681.9 litres a day, water is released from the Llyn Brianne dam. In 2011 a new water treatment plant was opened at Capel Dewi, supplied from Nantgaredig, to provide water for the Carmarthen area.

Nant y Ffin (Boundary Stream)

Nant y Ffin is a hamlet on the Abergorlech to Brechfa road in the beautiful Cothi valley. There are just a few houses with the old mill, on the Nant Y Ffin, by the bridge.

Newchurch

Newchurch or Eglwys Newydd is a tiny village west of the Gwili north of Carmarthen. Records show that in 1130, land at Eglwys Newydd was bestowed on the Priory at Carmarthen. The parish was an early centre of non-conformity, with nine dissenters recorded in 1676. The church was said to be one where "everything was out of repair", in 1672, following the English Civil War and Restoration of the Monarchy.

The present church dedicated to St Michael was built in 1829, replacing the nearby ruined church of Llanfiangel Croesfeini. Early Latin inscribed stones, known as the Severini and Curagni stones, were removed to the Carmarthen Museum at Abergwili. It is believed by some that the stones marked the site of a battle between the British and Romans. There are two Bronze Age round burial barrows in a field about three quarters of a mile east of Newchurch. They are accessible on a footpath opposite the barns now used as storage for Theatr Gendlaethol Cymru and marked Garn Fawr on the Ordnance Survey map. There is also, in an adjoining field, the earthwork of a Neolithic henge.

Newchurch was the birthplace of Bridget Bevan, in 1698, who was a major benefactor in support of Griffith Jones of Llanddowror and his 'circulating schools'.

New Inn

A hamlet centred on the cross roads of the A485 where it meets the Brechfa to Llanfiangel ar Arth road. The village flourished as a commercial centre with one of the main drove roads meeting the Carmarthen to Lampeter main road. At one time there were three public houses as well as the Travellers' Rest. With the coming of the railway to Pencader the trade slumped, and the village today has some sixty houses, a mixture of old and new, along the main road with a small modern estate off the Llanfihangel road, two engineering works and an agricultural machinery supplier.

As is not unusual, there is a chapel on the cross roads, Calvinistic Methodist, established in 1797 and rebuilt in 1832.

Pantyffynnon (Spring Valley)

Pantyffynnon is a village on the outskirts of Ammanford that sees the confluence of the Rivers Aman and Loughor and the junction of the Aman Valley and Heart of Wales Railways. The Llanelly Railway reached Pantyffynnon in 1839 and connections to the north and east followed. The station remains open for the Heart of Wales Line and the nearby signal box controls the line to the north as far as Craven Arms.

Next to the station was the Dinefwr Tinplate Works, established in 1880 and the last tinplate works in the valley to close in 1943. The old works were demolished in the 1970s and a smaller tinplate trading operation opened on the site.

Pantyffynnon drift mine opened in 1902, working up to four anthracite seams. It was a major employer in the area and, at the time of its closure in 1961, employed 596 men. Mining was carried on here much earlier as the proposal, as far back as 1770, to build a canal to transport the coal from Pantyffynnon to the navigable section of the Loughor shows.

Today the main road through the village is flanked by a variety of houses. There is an abundance of open countryside and woodland surrounding the village, with a suspension footbridge over the Aman on a path from the rugby ground. The Rivers Aman and Loughor meet just south of the station.

Pemberton

Now a suburb of Llanelli with 19th century terraced housing. The area is named after the Pemberton family who were prominent in mine owning and shipping in the early 19th century. It now has a major shopping development.

Pembrey (Welsh Pen Bre – Promontory Head)

Pembrey is a village on the A484 from Llanelli to Kidwelly, with a fascinating history. Just to the west of the village, in the woods as the ridge descending from Mynydd Pen Bre meets the road, are the remains of an Iron Age fort.

Early in the Norman invasion of Wales, Arnold le Botelier (later anglicised to Butler) was created Lord of the Manor of Pembrey. He built a manor house at Court Farm, immediately to the north of the village. Later, a 17th century mansion was built on the site and there are currently efforts to restore this partly derelict building. The estate passed to the Ashburnham family in the 17th century, marked by Ashburnham Road, Hotel and Golf Club. The family died out in the 1920s.

The church of St Illtyd was dedicated by Herewald, Bishop of Llandaff in 1066, though the present church dates from the 13th to the 15th centuries and has been fortunate in sympathetic Victorian restorations. It is one of the larger medieval churches in the county and has three bells dating from 1552. There is a 16th century timber barrelled roof and the crest of the Boteliers can be seen in the plasterwork. At the entrance to the church is a well preserved animal pound.

Through its early years Pembrey was a fishing village, but developed as a port with ships trading with La Rochelle in France in the latter part of the 16th century. In the latter part of the 18th century coal was mined on a small scale, and by 1810 a small iron industry had developed and a new harbour was built at Pembrey with a canal connecting to Kymer's Canal (see Carway). The harbour at Pembrey was subject to silting and a new harbour was built just to the east, known as Burry Port, which was to lead to the development of a town surrounding it. Pembrey harbour is still there but is now marshland and a wildlife habitat.

Industry continued but on a relatively small scale in Pembrey with the major industrial development in Burry Port.

Pembrey has an attractive village centre to the south of the main road and the church. There has been a considerable amount of modern development and there are two caravan parks. The village boasts one of the best golf courses in Wales – the Ashburnham, its own airport and motor racing circuit, a dry ski slope, miniature railway, forestry and eight miles of beach.

During World War II an airfield was built north-west of the village. Among the pilots who were based there were Guy Gibson, of Dambusters fame, and Ian Smith, the future Prime Minister of Southern Rhodesia. On the 23rd June, 1942, Oberleutnant Arnim Faber mistakenly landed his Focke-Wulf 190A, the latest German fighter, at Pembrey and was captured. There was also a high explosives factory.

The airfield is still in place catering for charter passenger flights, light aircraft and provides refuelling for the RAF. It operates 24 hours a day and there are plans for expansion.

The former airfield is also home to the National Motorsport Centre for Wales.

Pembrey Country Park has a mixture of forestry, dunes and beach in its 500 acres; in addition there is Pembrey Forest covering nearly 2500 acres. Cefn Sidan Sands is a Blue Flag beach offering safe bathing within the lifeguard patrolled areas with views across to the Gower peninsular. There is a cycle path, ski slope and toboggan run, a miniature railway and facilities for horse riding. Pembrey Forest is a nature reserve and is a dune forest containing no less than 35 species of butterfly, songbirds and birds of prey.

Wreckers are normally associated with Cornwall, but were active along the coast. On 21st November, 1828, the *Jeune Emma* a Cherbourg based ship of 400 tons bound for Le Havre from Martinique was wrecked on Cefn Sidan. Apparently the crew mistook the light from the Lundy lighthouse for that of Ushant. All but six of the crew died as did two of the passengers, Colonel Coquelin and his daughter, the niece of the Empress Josephine Napoleon. They were buried in the same grave at St Illtyd's, Pembrey. It is said that the lady's fingers were cut off by wreckers to retrieve her rings.

On March 2nd, 1827, the Carmarthen 173 ton schooner *New Comet* was wrecked on Cefn Sidan on her homeward voyage from London and, on June 5th, 1831, the Carmarthen sloop *Cresswell Castle* foundered off Pembrey.

Mat of the Iron Hand was a wrecker. He had lost a hand and had an iron hook. He used to tie lanterns to sheep along the dunes between Kidwelly and Pembrey to attract ships on to the sand banks. On one occasion one of the survivors was John Walter Vaughan, eldest son of Sir Walter Vaughan. Mat killed him and cut off his hand to get his gold signet ring. Mat was hanged.

Penboyr

Penboyr is a parish in north Carmarthenshire four miles south-east of Newcastle Emlyn. The derivation of the name is disputed, with some believing it is a corruption of Pen y Beirdd meaning chief of the bards. Others believe 'boyr' is derived from the Norse word for farm, giving its meaning the highest place on the farm. While others believe 'Boyr' is a corruption of Pyr who succeeded Sawyl Ben Uchel on the throne of Britain.

The church, dedicated to St Llawddog, while medieval in origin, had to be completely rebuilt in the 19th century. It stands alone save for the large Maes Llan Farm, some hundred yards away. The remains of the Tomen Llawddog motte and bailey castle stand in the field across the road from the church. The earliest record of the church is 1222 and it is thought that the church and castle are contemporary, possibly an attempt by the Anglo-Normans to establish a vill, but no settlement followed. The road leading to the church ends at Penrhiwficer, but further south is the site of an Iron Age fort.

Pencader (Promontory Fort)

Pencader owes its name to the Iron Age hill fort built at the head of the eastern ridge above the village.

Pencader is a large village in the valley of Afon Talog with the Nant Bele and Nant Gwen flowing into it. It is an old village with a motte and bailey castle constructed by Gilbert de Clare, 1st Earl of Pembroke in

1145. The motte remains behind the old school though the bailey disappeared under the railway. It was here that Henry II met the Lord Rhys in 1162 to receive homage. According to Giraldus Cambrensis, an old man when asked by Henry if Wales could ever be conquered, rfeplied "This nation, O King, may now, as in former times, be harassed, and in a great measure weakened and destroyed by your and other powers, and it will also prevail by its laudable exertions, but it can never be totally subdued through the wrath of man, unless the wrath of God shall concur. Nor do I think that any other nation than this of Wales, nor any other language, whatever may hereafter come to pass, shall on the day of severe examination before the Supreme Judge, answer for this corner of the earth." The event is commemorated on a plaque in the village with the Welsh text, situated opposite the Pavilion on the main road.

The church of St Mary was built on the site of the former chapel of ease in 1880-81 but has a 12th century font. Pencarreg is in the parish of Llanfiangel ar Arth.

For many centuries Pencarreg would have been a small village, but in 1864 the railway came in the form of the Carmarthen and Cardigan Railway. This met the Manchester and Milford Railway just north of Pencader. Neither of the lines were completed, with the Manchester and Milford line only running between Pencader and Strata Florida and the Carmarthen and Cardigan line stopping at Newcastle Emlyn. They meant, however, that Pencader was connected to Lampeter and Aberystwyth in the north, and from there through to the English Midlands and to Carmarthen in the south, and from there to Swansea, Cardiff and London. As a result Pencader grew, taking trade from nearby villages like New Inn. Passenger traffic continued until 1965 and freight until 1973.

Pencader is situated on the B4459, connecting Carmarthen and Llanybydder. The main road through the village consists of mainly late 19th and early 20th century development, but Castle Road, to the west, which leads to the church, has some attractive older cottages. Hen Capel or the Old Chapel is now a family centre.

Pencarreg (Stone Headland)

Pencarreg, named after the nearby mountain, is a small village on the A485 Lampeter to Llanybydder road. The Red Lion Inn has now sadly closed. The parish church of St Patrick is set above the village and the rocky outcrop north-east of the church explains the village name. The church is medieval in origin but was renovated in the 19th century, and retains a number of older features including a 12th century font. There is some evidence that the original dedication of the church was to St Padarn.

The village has a lake, Llyn Pencarreg, which is privately owned. It was formed following the Ice Age when a huge ice mass melted. It is nutrient poor but is an important wildfowl habitat. Such lakes are normally found in more mountainous regions and Llyn Pencarreg is a Site of Special Scientific Interest. It has no inflow or outflow and is believed to be fed by an artesian spring.

Until 1965 Pencarreg was a halt on the Lampeter to Carmarthen rail line and the line of the track is still visible, running between the road and the lake.

Pendine (Welsh Pentywyn – End of the Dunes)

Pendine is famous as the one time centre for world speed land records on its seven mile sands. Essentially there are two distinct parts to the village. Coming from the east the road is lined with caravan and chalet parks and the usual collection of sea front cafes. One slightly unusual feature is that car parking is allowed on the beach, which has particularly firm sand. Sir Malcolm Campbell and J G Parry Thomas both set World Records here in 1924-27. Parry Thomas was killed and his car *Babs* was buried in the sands, but has since been raised and restored. There is a Museum of Speed in the village which is home to *Babs*. In 1933, Amy Johnson and her husband, Jim Mollison, took off from the beach to fly to the United States in their De Haviland *Rapide*. They ran out of fuel and crash landed at Bridgeport Connecticut. The beach is seven miles long, although part is restricted due to Ministry of Defence testing.

The other part of the village is much older and sits on top of the hill. The Grade II listed church of St Margaret is medieval but was restored in 1869 by John Prichard. It has a saddle back tower and three 20th century stained glass windows. The dedication to St Margaret has led to some confusion as the nearby churches at Eglwys Cynym and Llandawke have similar dedications. This has been attributed to Sir Guy de Brian, Lord of Laugharne, who claimed descent from St Margaret of Scotland and whose niece was the local St Margaret Marlos.

Pendine Great House stands next to the church. Its first recorded occupier was William Barret in the early 16th century, but its origins are considered to be much earlier.

The residents of Pendine used to go early on Easter Sunday morning to the hill behind the Spring Well and threw stones into the sea to 'break Lent's neck' though the hill's name was corrupted to Break Land's Neck.

In the cliffs to the west of the entrance to the beach are caverns with a stream flowing into the sea.

Peniel

Named after its chapel, Peniel is an expanding village three miles north of Carmarthen on the A485. Besides the chapel and a few older houses in the centre of the village, the bulk of the housing is late 20th early 21st century, with a large new school opened in 2009.

To the west of the village in open fields are two standing stones, either side of the Nant Felys.

Penrherber (Head of a Leafy Glade)

A small farming hamlet situated on a crossroads south-west of Newcastle Emlyn. Housing is early 20th century or earlier with just one modern bungalow.

Penrhiwgoch

Penrhiwgoch is a small community centred around a cross roads on the B4297 between Gorslas and Dryslwyn. It consists of just 5 houses, the Particular Baptists Chapel of 1797 and Garngoch Farm. The name translates as 'Top of the Red Slope' and the earth locally is unusually red for Carmarthenshire, but Penrhiwgoch is a little past the top of the climb from the Towy valley. Properties to the east however refer to Allt-Rhiw-Moch, 'moch' referring to pigs.

Pensarn (Head of the Paved Road)

Pensarn today is Carmarthen's out-of-town shopping area with all the usual garages, supermarkets, garden centres and fast food outlets. Its history is more sinister. Prior to 1818, the public executions of county convicts took place here. Among them were Edwards of

Llandefaelog for pilfering in 1739; Edward Higgings for burglary in Laugharne in 1767; Will Mani for murdering a woman on Pendine Mountain, described as being 'gibbeted on the mountain' and Gutto Rowley (see Llanddarog) for murdering a tithe collector, both in 1788; Shoni'r Cornel, a shoemaker from Llanfiangel Abercowin, for murdering his father in 1797; and John Morris for horse stealing in 1804. The name refers to the Roman road that started here.

Pentre Cwrt (Grange Village)

Pentre Cwrt is a village in the north of the county, east of Llangeler. It was the site of a grange or farmstead belonging to the Cistercian Abbey of Whitland. It is thought to have been the abbot's summer residence. The grange chapel of St Mary became a chapel of ease after the Dissolution of the Monasteries under Henry VIII and was rebuilt by the Victorians. It stands about a mile east of the village on the road to Bancyffordd, It is almost certain that the site was used long before the Cistercians as there are fragments of a stone bearing the inscription 'Cabarbalom son of Brocagnus' in Latin and Ogham. The names are believed to be Irish in origin. The church, now under Llangeler, is still in use.

Near the church is Ffynnon Fair, a holy well but without public access. Opposite the church is Pencastell, the motte of a motte and bailey castle.

The village is attractive with two inns, the Black Horse and the Plas Parke, and modern housing - some up-market. The Afon Seidi flows through the village and used to power Henfryn Mill, on the road north past the Plas Parke, which also leads to Pont Allt y Cafan over the Teifi. Below the bridge is a weir and Alltcafan Mill which was in use until the latter part of the 20th century. Another mill in the village, the Derw, is now split into industrial units, but the village was once a major centre for the woollen trade, mainly flannel shirt production. This was aided by the building of a rail line from Llandysul to Newcastle Emlyn, with a halt at Pentre-Cwrt near the Allt y Cafan bridge. The first train left Llandysul for Newcastle Emlyn at 06.52 on 1st July, 1895. The line closed to passengers in 1952 and to freight in 1973.

Pentregwenlais (Gwenlais Village)

Pentregwenlais is a small village just north of Llandybie. The road through the village follows the line of Nant Gwenlais. The village today is peaceful with housing of mixed age. The area was a centre for limestone quarrying and to the north of the village is the lake of the disused Cilyrychen Quarry. To the south of the village a railway led from Pentregwenlais to Pont Lash, just north of Ammanford. Limestone kilns were numerous in the area and at the Pentregwenlais Quarry, north-west of the village, there was a bank of three kilns built in 1903. Much of the quarried areas has now been converted to a nature reserve.

Penybanc (Top of the Slope)

Penybanc is a village lying between Ammanford in the east and Tycroes and Saron in the west. Penybanc Road forms part of the A483 main road from Ammanford to the M4 and is a mixture of late 19th and early 20th century development with modern high density housing. Pisgah Baptist Chapel built in 1911, and Penybanc Rugby Club are on the A483. Parklands Road has a lower density of housing with the Newtown estate of bungalows off it. Today Penybanc is a suburb of Ammanford, but blessed with open spaces including the Allt Nant Y Ci Country Park, which offers superb views over Ammanford and the surrounding area. The country park was formed from the site of the old Saron colliery and Nant y Ci farm. Saron colliery was started by the Blaina Colliery Company in 1915. At its peak it employed 384 men. It closed in 1956.

Penybont (Bridgend)

Penybont is a hamlet in the parish of Trelech a'r Betws, set in the valley of the Dewi Fawr. The bridge crossing the stream is Grade II listed Trelech Bridge. On one side of the valley stands Penybont Independent Chapel while up the hill on the other side of the valley is St Teilo's, the parish church of Trelech a'r Betws. At the bottom of the valley is an old mill and next to the bridge is the village school; altogether a delightful, remote and unspoilt hamlet.

Penygroes (Top Cross)

Penygroes is a former mining village between Llandybie and Cross Hands. It is perhaps best known as the headquarters of the Apostolic Church which was established in the village in 1916 and remained until 2003, when it moved to Swansea. The Apostolic Church International Bible School was established in the village in 1933. The Apostolic Church is a Pentecostal church with its origins in the great Welsh religious revival of 1904-5. From its roots in Wales the church has spread worldwide with a membership of 4.5 million in Nigeria alone. The Bible College was used in 2011 by a Korean church. The Temple is in Bryncwar Road and the College in Bryn Road.

The first Independent chapel in Penygroes opened in 1823 with a second in 1825. In 1840, the Penygroes Temperance Society joined with societies in Betws, Hendre and Llandybie to form a Temperance Union.

John Aeron Thomas, the son of a Cardiganshire farmer, started the Emlyn Colliery in 1883. Initially a slant mine it was abandoned in 1892 in favour of two drift mines. At its height in the mid 1920s, the colliery employed 760 men. It closed in 1939 though in more recent years the village has seen open cast mining. This has now been completed and the land is being restored.

Penymynydd (Mountain Top)

Penymynydd is a modern development on the road between Llanelli and Trimsaran. In addition to housing along the main road, there are small estates on both sides.

Pontargothi (Cothi Bridge)

Pontargothi or Cothi Bridge is a village on the A40 where it crosses the River Cothi. Originally there was a ford at this point. There are three inns, all on the Llandeilo side of the river and the Salutation, dating from the 17th century, lays claim, with its eight resident ghosts, to being the most haunted pub in Wales. The Cresselly Arms takes its name from a nineteenth century local landowner, John Hensleigh Allen of Cresselly Pembrokeshire, who purchased Cefn y Coed, now known as Kincoed, in 1839. The house was originally owned by the descendants of Grono Goch, Constable of Dryslwyn Castle and dates from the 15th century.

The village originally came under the parish of neighbouring Llanegwad but in 1868 an Englishman, Henry James Bath, came to Pontargothi and built Alltyferin House on the eastern side of the Cothi north of the village and wanted to worship in an Anglican church in English. Having made his money in the copper industry in Swansea (the town was nicknamed Copperopolis) he decided to build his own church and no expense was spared. The result was Holy Trinity Church about half a mile north of the village on the Carmarthen bank of the river. He built a bridge to enable him and his family to walk to the church from Alltyferin House, though the bridge is no longer in existence. Holy Trinity Church however is one of the hidden gems of the county. Never having been granted a licence for burials, the church is set in a field and used, as I discovered on my first visit, as a car park during weddings and funerals. The church is a mixture of Gothic and Romanesque styles designed by Benjamin Bucknall, an architect influenced by Eugene Emmanuel Viollet Le Duc, the restorer of Notre Dame de Paris. The exterior is relatively plain, and very reminiscent of the English church in Zermatt, but the interior, recently restored, is magnificent, richly decorated with scenes from the Bible while the pulpit is made from Swansea marble. The rich windows contain Clayton and Bell stained glass. Clayton and Bell were based in Regent Street and provided stained glass windows for Norwich Cathedral, Truro Cathedral, the West Window of King's College Cambridge, Peterborough Cathedral, and St James Cathedral Toronto as well as churches in New York and Sydney. Their windows used medieval techniques of colouring glass that gave a greater luminosity than many of their contemporaries. The walls are decorated with 25 panels illustrating biblical stories drawn by A Stansell of Taunton, a firm still in existence. In anticipation of the decoration, Bucknall installed a larger than usual wall cavity that has ensured that there has been no damage from damp.

The church did however have a coal boiler and over the years the paintings became soiled by smoke. A restoration was undertaken in 2006-7, bringing the church back to its pristine glory. Apart from the paintings, the walls and barrel ceiling are all richly decorated. The church is open on Thursday afternoons in summer between 2 and 4 pm, when visitors are greeted with tea and biscuits. Henry James Bath died before the church was completed and, with the lack of a licence for burial, the family vault under the church remains empty. Alltyferin House was demolished in the 1950s.

A mile north-east of the church is a motte of a motte and bailey castle overlooking the river. It is on private land but a footpath leading to a bridge across the Cothi passes beneath it.

Pontarsais (Englishman's Bridge)

Pontarsais is a hamlet on the A485 north of Carmarthen. The bridge crosses the Gwili river.

On the B4301 is the Gwili Pottery, a studio pottery open to visitors.

The Stag and Pheasant is a roadside inn, but last time I passed it was on the market.

Pont Henri (Henry's Bridge)

The derivation of the name is unclear. Thomas Morgan in his 1912 edition of *The Place Names of Wales* suggests that it was probably named after the bridge's builder. There seems to have been a tendency to name bridges in this vicinity, with Pontyates and Pont Andrew.

Pont Henri is a former mining village in the Gwendraeth Fawr valley with the larger part of the village lying to the north-west of the Ponyberem to Pontyates road. The village has a mixture of housing, mainly from the late 19th and early 20th century, but beyond the bridge to the north-west is a development of modern individual properties.

Industry came early to Pont-Henri with a furnace to smelt iron ore established certainly by 1611, but possibly earlier. Remains can be seen today on the west bank of the river. A poem suggests that a successful furnace was established by a Swedish ironmaster in Elizabethan times. This is probable as cannonballs were in demand for the war against Spain. The nearby Baltic Inn alludes to the Swedish connection. The first documented owner was Hugh Grundy who had a dispute over water rights with Walter Vaughan of Llanelli, which led to the water supplying power to the furnace to be cut and temporary closure.

The Ponthenry Colliery Company was set up in 1865 and operated three drift mines. At its peak it employed over 800 men, but while there were plenty of reserves it became too dangerous to operate and closed in 1936.

Kymer's Canal that had connected Kidwelly and Carway was extended by 1830 to Pont Henri and on to Pontyberem. Rather than locks to raise boats from one level to another, they used inclined planes, movng the barge on to a rail track and pulling it up. This explains the name of the Incline Inn in Pont Henri.

The canal was replaced by the railway which eventually reached Cwm Mawr at the foot of Tumble. Passenger traffic on the railway ceased in 1953 and freight in 1996. Plans are afoot to re-open part of the line between Pont-newydd and Pontyberem with a station at Pont Henri, though the track beyond Pontyates is now a heritage footpath.

Pontyates (Welsh spelling Pont-iets)

The original name was Trewiail, the Place of Rods, but there is some dispute as to the derivation of Pontyates. Some attribute it to a bridge built by a Mr Yates while others allude to the toll gate near the bridge and this would give Pont-iets or Bridge Gates.

A former mining village on the road between Llanelli and Carmarthen, Pontyates is the junction of the road leading from Cross Hands and the M4 to Ffos Las Racecourse. It is an elongated village, some two miles in length, built across the valley of the Gwendraeth Fawr.

There were two collieries in the area, the Gwendraeth and the Plasbach, though they were to be linked below ground. The first to open was the Plasbach in 1856 and it worked three seams through two shafts, one 400 feet deep. The Gwendraeth, which was just outside the village, opened in the latter years of the 19th century and worked just one seam, the Carway Fawr, and was a single drift. Both pits closed in 1928.

The church of St Mary dates from 1910-12 and replaced the older church which still retains the graveyard further up the road towards Carmarthen. Three walls of the old church remain, a feature within the churchyard, and recent burials have taken place within the walls.

The rail track to the south of Pontyates is now designated the Pontiets Mining Heritage Trail.

Pontyates was the birthplace of Mandy Rice Davies, who hit the headlines in the 1960s over the Profumo affair. *Eastenders'* actress June Brown was evacuated here in World War II.

Pontyberem (Bridge at the Mouth of the Beran)

Pontyberem is a former mining village in the valley of the Gwendraeth Fawr. The old name of the village was Pontyherw or Robbery Bridge.

It is a large village with one of the routes from Llanelli to Carmarthen crossing the Pontyates to Cross Hands, Gwendraeth Valley road. Housing is mixed and there are a number of local shops including a supermarket housed in the old cinema.

Ponyberem was connected to Kidwelly and then Pembrey harbours by canal and then rail. Part of the main road is named Station Road. Passenger trains stopped in 1953, but coal trains continued until 1996. There are plans to reopen part of the line between Pont Newydd and Pontyberem.

There were four collieries in the village: the Pontyberem Colliery, started in 1845, The Gwendraeth, the Pentremawr and the Glynhebog. The Gwendraeth Colliery was purchased by brothers Daniel and Alfred Watney, the latter described as an iron and coal master from Wandsworth in London who married Helen Raby of the Llanelli industrialist family. In 1852 disaster struck when the mine was flooded and 26 men died. There is a memorial to the disaster in the village. A second shaft was dug from the Coalbrook estate, the home of Alfred and Helen Watney, and continued in production until 1910 by which time the Glynhebog Colliery had taken over. The Watneys started the Gwendraeth Iron Works in 1854. Pentremawr was the largest of the collieries in Pontyberem and was the last to close in 1974.

Much of the coal from Pontyberem was shipped to Cornwall and Cornish sandstone shipped back as ballast was used to build St John's Church in 1893, and indeed large parts of the village.

Coalbrook House was one of the oldest houses in the area, being built in 1670 with a thatched roof. The staircase was of Italian origin and part has been preserved in Carmarthen County Museum. In the 1940s attempts were made to restore the house but it was eventually demolished and replaced by a split level Nordic style house.

Porthyrhyd (Ford Entrance)

Porthyrhyd is a small village originally on the main A48 trunk road but now by-passed. It contains two pubs and the Bethlehem Chapel, rebuilt in 1842. Opposite the chapel stands the Chapel Schoolroom built in 1893. The burial ground appears to have a large number of pillared memorials.

The unusually titled Abadam Arms is named after the owner of nearby Middleton Hall (now the National Botanic Garden of Wales), Edward Abadam, or Ab Adam denoting the son of Adam. A relief of Edward Abadam in wax, by David Morrison, is on display in the Victoria and Albert Museum.

Pumsaint (Five Saints) (The Roman Luentinum)

Pumsaint is a small village on the A482 and takes its name from a stone. Legend had it that, while on a pilgrimage, five saints, Gwyn, Gwynno, Gwynnoro, Cilynin and Ceitho rested on the stone in a storm (one on each face and one on top) and the indentations mark where their heads lay. The devil had come along and caused the heads to be embedded in the stone until they were freed by Merlin, King Arthur's legendary magician.

In reality the stone, known as Carreg Pumsaint, is believed to have been used as an anvil for ore crushing and would have lain on its side in the Roman Gold Mines at Dolaucothi. The existence of the Roman mines was unknown for 1500 years, so in a time when there was a strong belief in miracles, it is not surprising that the story of the five saints gained credence.

The Dolaucothi Gold Mine is now owned by the National Trust and is a major tourist attraction. I first heard about the mines in the 1960s while studying at Lampeter. Handel Evans, owner of the Mile End Café described the working conditions in the 1930s and the fact that flooding caused the abandonment of mining activity in 1938. Although mining resumed in the 19th century, it was only in 1935 that the Roman origins of the mines was realised and even then the extent of Roman activity in the area was not fully comprehended. Field surveys in 1975 and later have revealed the vast scale of the operations carried out by the Romans.

Initially, the Romans would have panned for gold in the River Cothi and other streams, but their preferred method was hydraulic mining, whereby water was used to wash away the surface to reveal the gold veins. They built a series of leats, tanks and aqueducts to bring water to and store it on the site. The longest of the aqueducts is seven miles. There was underground mining by the Romans too and it is likely that they used water wheels to pump water out of the mines.

Evidence of pottery and other finds in the vicinity showed that Romans mined here for at least 300 years, though the Roman fort which lies under the village of Pumsaint was abandoned during the 2nd century.

The mines are now open as a visitor attraction with a museum on site together with 20th century machinery. Visitors can take an underground tour and pan for gold.

The village of Pumsaint is small. The Dolaucothi Hotel is closed but there are plans to refurbish and re-open the hotel.

Pwll (Pool)

Pwll is a village between Llanelli and Burry Port. The main street is of terraced houses but further west housing is restricted to the north of the road with views across to north Gower. The Millennium Coastal Path and the Llanelli to Carmarthen rail line are also to the south of the village.

There were two woollen mills in Pwll, Waun Eos started in 1874 and Pont yr Odin in 1906. Waun Eos ceased production before World War I but Pont yr Odin continued until 1957.

To the north-east of the village is Stepney Park Nursing Home. Formerly the property was known as Cilymaenllwyd (Seat of the Grey Rock). In the 16th century the property was owned by the Lloyd family, who claimed descent from Urien Rheged, Prince of Rheged and Lord of Gower, the house passed through a number of families until purchased in 1911 by Sir Edward and Lady Stafford Howard. They rebuilt the mansion which remained in the family until 1965 when it was purchased by the local authority and converted into a nursing home. It is now privately owned.

The church of Holy Trinity Pwll was opened in 1904 on land donated by architect Cyril Arengo Jones, the then owner of Cilymaenllwyd, who also designed the church. The establishment of the church was largely due to the enthusiasm of the local policeman, John Rees. Rees started by holding services in the police station to establish the demand for the church and over 300 attended the Service of Dedication, most of whom were unable to get into the small church.

Pwll Trap (Trap Pool)

Pwll Trap is a community now by-passed by the A40 west of St Clears. The older part of the village developed along the old A40 with the White Lion inn, now doubling as village shop. There has been considerable modern development including high density housing.

Bethlehem Independent Chapel was established circa 1696, the first independent chapel in the area of St Clears.

Red Roses

The romantically named Red Roses is a small village at a cross roads on the A477 St Clears to Pembroke Dock road. The village pub, the

Llwyngwair Arms has been renamed the Sporting Chance. The village forms part of the parish of Eglwys Cymyn.

Rhandirmwyn (Area of Ores)

Rhandirmwyn is a village in the beautiful, but remote, upper Towy valley, below the massive Llyn Brianne dam. The village today is rural with its pub the Royal Oak and St Barnabus Church, down the lane opposite the Royal Oak, but for hundreds, possibly thousands of years it was the centre of a major mining operation. The two Nant y Mwyn mines situated to the north-east of the village produced vast quantities of lead and zinc. It is believed the Romans may have mined here; their gold mine at Dolaucothi is only ten miles away. Written records start in 1304, but the peak of mining came in the 18th and 19th centuries when Cornish managers were brought in, and up to 400 men women and children where employed in the mining operations. Cliffe in *The book of South Wales, the Bristol channel, Monmouthshire and the Wye* of 1848 reported that 180 men and 30 women and boys were employed. The mines produced huge profits for the Cawdors of Golden Grove before they closed in 1932.

The church of St Barnabus was built in 1877 to a design by John Loughborough Pearson, best known for Truro Cathedral, with monies provided by the Earl of Cawdor. The church has a bellcote but no tower or steeple.

The countryside around Rhandirmwyn is one of the last strongholds of the indigenous oak and therefore populated with the flora and fauna that thrive in open woodland.

Rhandirmwyn is home to Coleg Elidyr, a specialist college for 18-25 year olds with learning difficulties.

A comparatively large number of former Rhandirmwyn miners emigrated to the United States and two in particular were successful, both in industry and politics. Morgan B Williams, a Republican, became a member of the US House of Representatives for Pennsylvania, and John T Williams, also a Republican, was elected to the State Senate of Pennsylvania.

Rhos (Moor)

Rhos is a village on the A484 with a mixture of modern housing and a few old cottages. Part of the village lies to the east of the main road, with Tremle, the old smithy, on the road that runs parallel to the A484. The village church, St James, dates from the early 20th century and there is an Evangelical church and an Independent Chapel.

Rhosaman (Aman Moor)

The name describes the location perfectly. The hamlet is on the road between Brynaman and Cefnbrynbrain and was the site of one of the earliest coal mines in the Aman Valley. John Jones acquired the Blaengurwen Colliery at Rhosaman in 1802, though there is evidence of earlier mining in the form of bell pits north of the village. Early coal extraction was for the use of burning lime to use as fertilizer on farms. The recreation ground stands on the site of the old colliery with a memorial to the seven miners who were killed in an explosion in 1924.

Rhosaman has an independent chapel, Bethania, and the Rose and Crown Hotel. The River Aman flows through the village next to the hotel. To the south of the village are extensive open cast mining activities.

Rhosmaen (Stone Point)

Rhosmaen is a community on the A40 just to the north of Llandeilo. Largely a ribbon development, there are some attractive older cottages but the village has mainly modern housing. There was a tannery at the northern end of Rhosmaen but this has recently been demolished. The most prominent building is the Plough Hotel which has been considerably enlarged over the last twenty years.

Rhosmaen House is situated to the north of the village and main road. A large Victorian house, it was the home of Dr David Morgan CB, MD St And, Inspector General RN. Morgan was born in Rhosmaen in 1823 and, after qualifying as a doctor, entered the Royal Navy. He served across the world including the Crimea War and with land forces in China. He became Inspector General of Fleets and Hospitals, the highest medical rank in the Royal Navy and shortly before his death, in 1893, was appointed Physician in Ordinary to Queen Victoria.

The Heart of Wales Railway runs to the east of the village, as does the River Towy.

Rhydargaeau (Rhyd – ford; argaeu – dam, weir or embankment)

Rhydargaeau is a village on the A485 north of Carmarthen. A mainly modern ribbon development, there are a number of older houses around the centre of the village with its two chapels. The source of the Nant Brechfa is just beside the road.

Rhydcymerau (Ford at the Confluence of Rivers)

Rhydcymerau is situated in a beautiful spot on the Afon Melinddwr and Nant Moelen. Entering from the south on the B4337 Llansawel to Llanybydder road, there are attractive older cottages as you cross the bridge. But the village pub, the Red Dragon with its caravan and campsite, and post office are closed and the slate clad Calvinistic Methodist Chapel is in need of repair. The village primary school closed in January 2012, altogether a depressing picture of rural life. Rhydycymerau has expanded with new housing to the north and on the Llidiad-Nenog road, but the newcomers appear to have failed to sustain the social life of the village.

In the 18th and early 19th centuries the village was on one of the principal drovers' routes and was the site of a cattle shoeing compound.

Rhydcymerau was the home of David John Williams, the Welsh nationalist and writer. He was one of the founders of Plaid Cymru in 1925 and spent nine months in Wormwood Scrubs after taking part in the setting fire to the bombing school at Penyberth in 1936. He wrote about the village, where he died in 1970 at the age of 84 in the arms of Gwynfor Evans minutes after speaking in the village chapel where he is buried. His home near the village was Aber Nant Farm and a plaque celebrates his time there.

Rhydcymerau was the subject of an evocative poem by Gwenallt, David James Jones, who had spent his childhood holidays in the village. In the poem he decries the forestation of the area, calling the Forestry Commission the 'English Minotaur'.

To the south of the village is a forestry picnic site called Abernant.

Rhydywrach – see Henllanfallteg

Saint Ishmael – see Ferryside

Salem

Set in rural Carmarthenshire, north of Llandeilo, Salem village takes its name from the listed Independent Chapel built in 1817. The village has a number of older cottages but is mainly a modern development, with the Angel Inn opposite the chapel.

A mile north-east of Salem is Maes y Castell, the remains of a small iron age fort, offering views to the south over the Towy valley. There is evidence of a round house and Maes y Castell may have been the Iron Age equivalent of a fortified manor.

Sandy

Sandy is a village between Llanelli and Burry Port. It was the site of the Llanelly Steelworks. Production ceased in 1981 and the village has seen the development of Sandy Water Park, new housing around Sandpiper Road and the Sandpiper family pub and restaurant.

Sandy Road is the main thoroughfare and is lined with early 20th century terraced housing.

To the north of the village stood Stradey Park, the celebrated Llanelli Rugby ground, which was sold for housing when the new Parc y Scarlets stadium was developed.

Saron, SA44

Saron is a village on a cross roads on the A484 south of Llangeler. The village has a mixture of older cottages and modern bungalows set in open countryside on a ridge between the valleys of the Nant Wthan and the Camnant. Saron Chapel, which gives the village its name, was originally Penlon Chapel Drefach, but the appointment of David Davies as minister in 1790 meant that the old chapel was too small and Saron was built in 1792. Davies moved to Swansea in 1795 and had continued success. He was the writer of some 80 hymns, some of which are still used today. The A484 was originally a turnpike road built in the 1790s. By 1839 there were just four buildings in the village. The village has a hostelry, the Llwyndafydd Inn and a golf course.

Saron, Ammanford

Saron is a former mining village west of Ammanford. Named after its chapel, Saron today has a predominance of post war and modern housing, with relatively few properties dating from before 1930. Saron Colliery was started in 1915 by the Blaina Colliery Company. At its peak it employed 384 men. It closed in 1956. The colliery was situated at the eastern end of the village and the site now forms part of the Allt Nant y Ci Country Park.

St David's Parish church is a modern red brick building with an unusual squat castellated tower

Swiss Valley

Swiss Valley is a large modern housing development north of Felinfoel. It is to the east of the road to Llannon whereas the reservoirs which formed the 'Swiss Valley' are to the west.

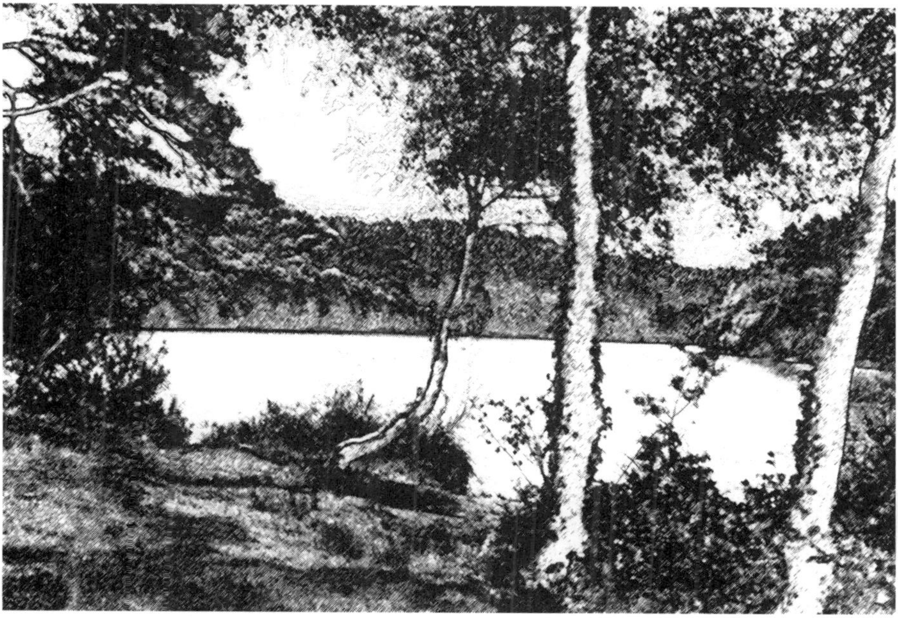

Felindre, Swiss Valley

Taliaris (The top of the place where there are flocks of hens)

Taliaris is an estate rather than a village. Grade I listed Plas Taliaris was built in 1638 by a branch of the Gwynne family. It was remodelled and refronted around 1780, and was purchased by Lord Robert Seymour in 1787 and became his principal residence. The third son of the 1st Marquess of Hertford, Seymour was a soldier and politician. He served in the American War of Independence and for five years served as Lieutenant-Colonel Commandant of the 2nd Battalion, Carmarthenshire Volunteers. He was a Member of Parliament for a number of constituencies including Carmarthenshire, which he represented for 13 years. He financed the building of the north transept and a vicarage for Taliaris Chapel. He was known for his philanthropy, in particular with regard to slaves and lunatics. He died in 1831 just before his 83rd birthday.

In 1830 Seymour sold Taliaris to William Henry Peel, a member of a family of Lancashire industrialists founded by 'Parsley' Peel, so called because of the parsley design on his cotton products. The Peel family included Sir Robert Peel, the founder of the police and Prime Minister. Peel married Anna Maria Lloyd of the old Welsh family of that name. The Peel family lived at Plas Taliaris until the 1950s, since when it has had a chequered history.

The Plas is now owned by a community which believes in "the practice of mindfulness in daily life" and offers courses and retreats.

Warren Cottage refers to the old rabbit warren in the woodland which would have been used to supply the Plas with a ready supply of meat. The woods which contain a lake have been sold off from the estate.

Taliaris chapel was a chapelry attached to Llandeilo. It was rebuilt in 1660 by William Gwynne, with the addition of a north transept by Lord Seymour. It was rebuilt in 1892 by Herbert Peel, the then owner of Plas Taliaris, and was consecrated as Holy Trinity Church. The church is on the B4302 and offers views over the Dulais valley.

A short distance south of the church on the opposite side of the road is the Taliaris War Memorial. Among others it commemorates two sons of Herbert Peel, Alan Ralph Peel who was killed in action at Karonga in South Africa in 1914 and Robert Lloyd Peel MC who died of wounds suffered in the Battle of Passchendaele in 1917. Donated by the Peel family, the memorial is impressive with an inset marble cross and the names of the fallen on marble tablets.

Talley (Tal y Llychau – Head of the Lakes)

Talley is a small village north of Llandeilo, dominated by the ruins of Talley Abbey. There are two distinct areas of the village; part is a ribbon development along the main Llandeilo to Lampeter road, while

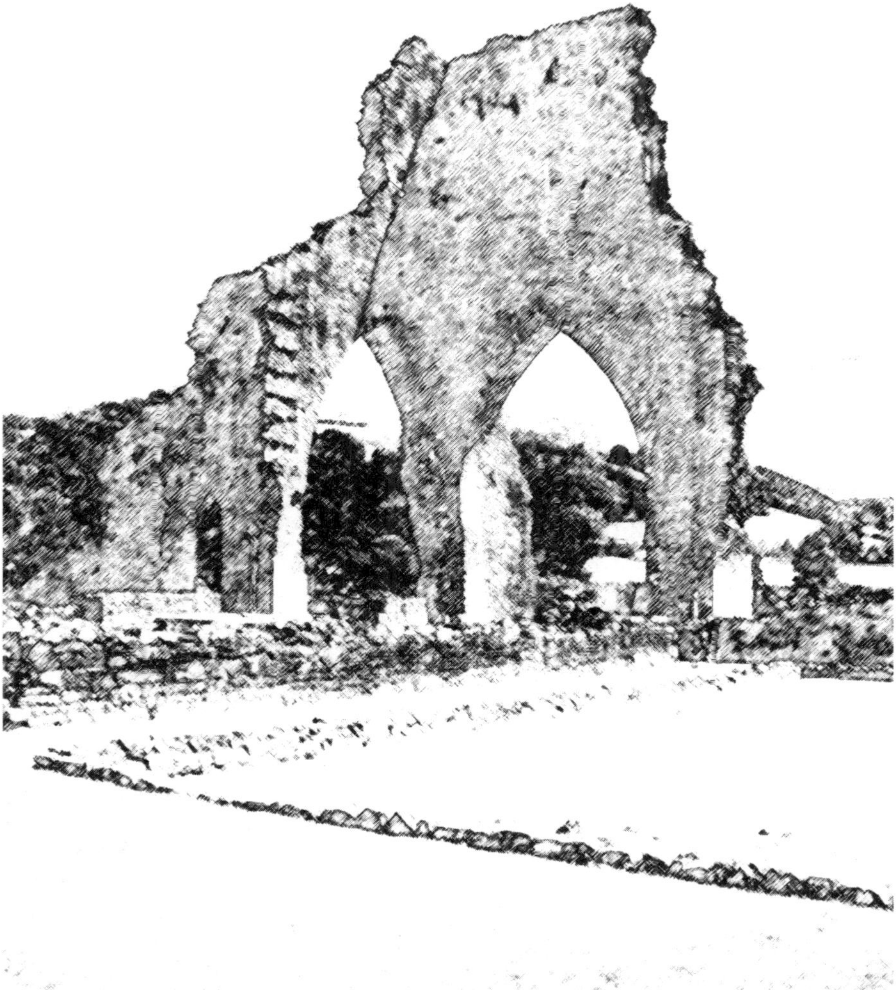

Talley Abbey

the other older, more peaceful part leads to the church and Abbey ruins. Founded in 1185 on land granted by Lord Rhys, the Abbey of the Blessed Virgin and St John the Baptist was the only abbey in Wales run by the Premonstratensians or White Canons monastic order. Set in a valley under tree clad hills, the abbey ruins have a special attraction. Not as large or impressive as Tintern or even Strata Florida, Talley abbey was never completed. The site is open to the public free of charge. The outline of the medieval church is visible, as are remnants of north and east walls of the tower. The Abbey was built on a precise location, so the rain draining from the north roof fed into the lakes and then into the River Cothi, while water from the south roof fed into the Afon Ddu and then into the Towy. After the dissolution of the monasteries, the church remained in use as the parish church but fell into decay. It was rebuilt in the Grecian style in 1773, dedicated to St Michael and the Angels, using stone from the old abbey.

On Dissolution, the abbey was transferred to the owners of Abermarlais, Llansadwrn.

Beyond the church of St Michael are the two lakes that give Talley its Welsh name. Between the lakes are the remains of Talley Castle, a motte some 15 foot high and 24 feet in diameter.

The lakes, glacial in origin, were used by the monks of the abbey for fish farming but now form a Site of Special Scientific Interest and a nature reserve. There is a hide for bird watching between the lakes.

The village eventually came under the Edwinsford estate.

Talog (Pediment)

Set in a wooded valley in the heart of rural Carmarthenshire, Talog is a delightful village. At its centre is an agricultural supplies merchant and perhaps most surprisingly a village store. Talog YMCA has a large hall used by the villagers and the surrounding communities.

In the first part of the 19th century toll roads were the norm in Carmarthenshire, but there was widespread fraud by the trustees responsible for the roads and tolls. One member of the Carmarthen and Lampeter Trust took the profits from some improvements and built himself a wall at Talog, though this was destroyed by rioters. The Rebecca riots began at Efailwen in 1839 (see Efailwen). Talog men took part in the 1843 Rebecca Riots at Carmarthen and were fined by the magistrates. Constables were sent to the village to levy the fines, but were forced to return, unable to serve the warrants. 30 pensioners were then sworn in to help enforce the warrants and seized goods belonging to a Mr Harries. On their return trip to Carmarthen, however, they were surrounded by 400 Rebecca armed supporters and after shots being fired in the air the constables and pensioners returned to Carmarthen empty handed.

Talog is home to a very special health spa, attracting celebrity guests, including Michel Roux's spaniel and Frank Lampard's bulldog. The Dog House is very much an upmarket boarding kennels and training establishment for dogs.

Temple Bar

Temple Bar is a community on the A476 Llandeilo to Cross Hands road, centred on the Temple Bar Inn. Housing is almost exclusively modern.

Trapp

Trapp, or Trap as it is spelt locally, is an attractive village in the foothills of the Black Mountain above Llandeilo and Ammanford. The derivation of the name is unclear. It may be that there was a fish trap on the river or, as the valley is known as Cwm Lladron or 'Robbers' Valley', it may have been known as a place where traps were sprung. The River Cennen flows through the village which retains its pub, the Cennen. The village's main attraction is perched on a rocky outcrop above it.

Carreg Cennen Castle has probably the most dramatic setting of any castle in Wales. Dylan Thomas in *Under Milk Water* refers to "Carreg Cennen, King of time". It is visible from miles around. The path from the car park, through Castell Farm, climbs up to the north side of the castle, but the southern walls of the castle stand on the edge of a 200 foot cliff above the River Cennen. Roman coins have been found on the site, but it is believed that the first castle was built by the local Welsh princes of Deheubarth. The ruins today date from the 13th century and the castle was made unfit for purpose by demolition in 1462 after the Wars of the Roses. The entrance to the keep was a classic example of defensive castle architecture, with any invading force led through a series of turns and across drawbridges while under fire from the defenders, before reaching the main entrance. The window frames that remain in the southern wall are large,

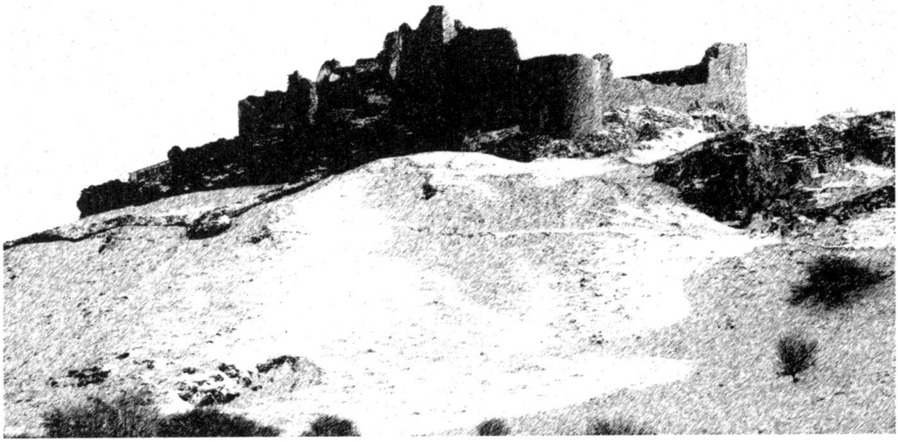

Carreg Cennen Castle, Trap

showing that the builders believed the castle was virtually impregnable from that side.

The castle offers superb views over the Black Mountain and a series of cairns can be seen on the crest of the Mountain to the south.

There is a path leading down from the castle and across the other side of the valley where the River Loughor gushes from a cave in the hillside. Known as Llygad Llwchwr or 'Eye of the Loughor', the cave system has never been fully explored. The stream flows very close to the Cennen which feeds the Towy at Llandeilo.

Not far from Llygad Llwchwr is Cwrt Bryn y Beirdd (Bards' Hill Court), one of the oldest surviving houses in Carmarthenshire, with features dating back to the 14th century. The origins of the house are unknown, but it is thought it may have been a more comfortable home for the residents of the castle in times of peace. It was the home of Hugh Fychan, the founder of the Vaughan dynasty of Golden Grove. The Cwrt is still inhabited and is a working farm.

Just to the south of the track leading from the Cwrt are the remains of the medieval Capel Dewi.

To the south of the village of Trap are the springs that supply Brecon Carreg Water.

Trelech a'r Betws

Trelech a'r Betws is an extensive parish eight miles north-west of Carmarthen, set in open farmland. The meaning of the name is open to debate. 'Tre' is village, 'llech' is stone, possibly referring to the druidic influence in the area; others think it means hidden village. 'A'r Betws' simply means near the oratory or almshouse. It is situated between the valleys of the Rivers Cywyn and Cynin with the Dewi Fawr running through it. The parish church of St Teilo is some three miles south-west of the village of Trelech, alongside a farm in Penybont, while Betws, the site of a ruined chapel of ease, is one and a quarter miles south of Trelech.

The parish church was rebuilt in 1834, but is on the site of a Celtic Llan. Capel Betws is now a dangerous ruin on private land. For a chapel of ease it was a sizeable building, but church services ceased in 1710.

The village of Trelech, on the B4299, is attractive with older buildings at the centre and the Tafarn Beca.

Crugebolion Common was fenced but Rebecca and 200 of her followers led by men on horseback assembled one morning and removed all the hedges and the common to the west of the village of Trelech has remained open ever since.

Crug y Dyrn or Crug y Dryn was, according to 19th century reports, a massive cairn, 180 feet high and 210 feet in circumference. Today it is just 10 foot high but still clearly visible from the road to Alma and Pandy, off the B4299. It was apparently hollow in the centre with a large flat stone covering a cist. According to legend a dragon or gwiber protects this cairn.

Trimsaran

A former mining village in the Gwendraeth valley, Trimsaran is translated as Ridge Way, but legend has it that it takes its name from a very early mansion of that name. By the 17th century Trimsaran was the home to a branch of the Vaughan family of Golden Grove.

Trimsaran today is a large commuter village on the B4308 Llanelli to Kidwelly road to the north of Mynydd Pembre. Housing is mainly post World War II though there are some terraced early 20th century houses in the lower part of the village. It is in the parish of Pembrey.

Coal had been mined in Trimsaran for hundreds of years, but it was the late 19th and early 20th centuries that saw a massive expansion. In 1896 there were 144 men employed in the Trimsaran Colliery. The colliery had three drift shafts, the Caedean, Waunhir and Upper Slant, employing 198 men by 1908. All three mines were connected underground. In 1931, Trimsaran employed 700 men but the work on these seams ended in 1934 and a new slant was dug, the Waunffynhonnau, employing 300 men in 1945. Mining ended in the village in 1954 with miners being transferred to the nearby Carway colliery. The area between Trimsaran and Carway then became the largest opencast mining operation in Europe before the area was reclaimed and is now the Ffos Las Racecourse.

The village is large enough to sustain a number of local shops and a leisure centre.

Tumble

Tumble is a sizeable former mining village between Cross Hands and Llanelli. It is split between Upper and Lower Tumble.

Upper Tumble runs along the A476 and has a good amount of modern housing. Lower Tumble follows the B4310, descending towards Cwm Mawr. The main part is terraced housing from the late 19th and early 20th century with newer properties further down the hill. The village has a number of local shops.

Tumble developed to provide homes for the miners in the Great Mountain Colliery which started in 1887. It was one of the largest and most productive mines in the area, employing 700 men in 1892 and 1,200 at its peak. It was closed in 1962. The much smaller Dynant Fach Colliery survived until 1998.

Tumble was on the Llanelly and Mynydd Mawr Railway that connected Ammanford, Cross Hands and Llanelli, much of which is now a cycleway. At the bottom of the village is the Mynydd Mawr Woodland Park, created on the site of old workings.

The area was originally agricultural and John Hughes of Ty Isaf Farm was a leader of the Rebecca Riots in the area after he was charged 1s/8d in tolls for an 8d load of lime. He was arrested and sentenced to 20 years transportation.

The religious revival of the early 20th century had an impact on Tumble, which had no less than nine non-conformist chapels. St David's Church was built between 1925 and 1928.

The name Tumble is taken from a local inn, the Tumbledown Dick, named after the nickname of Oliver Cromwell's son Richard.

Twynllanan

Twynllanan is a hamlet near Llanddeusant to the north of the Black Mountain. The village has views across to the Black Mountain. According to legend, Llanddeusant church was originally situated in Twynllanan, but miraculously moved overnight to Llanddeusant. 'Twyn' is Welsh for a hillock and 'llan' might denote a church ground. There is a Calvinistic Methodist Chapel which was established in 1742 with subsequent enlargements and a graveyard.

Tycroes (House on the Crossroads)

Tycroes is a former mining village at the western end of the Aman Valley. The industry was late in developing and in 1900 there were fewer than 100 houses. The development of the Wernos Colliery in 1903 saw a dramatic change in the village though the colliery itself had a chequered history. By 1938 it employed 432 men; it closed in 1940 to become a mining training centre, reopening in 1953 and increasing its manpower to 524 before closing in 1965, though some work continued on the surface until 1998. The nearby Rhos Colliery started in the 1860s and eventually linked with the Wernos but closed in 1938.

The first chapels were built in 1876 to be followed by St Edmund's Church in 1914.

The village has expanded rapidly, especially in the last 30 years of the 20th century, with a small shopping area and the Mountain Gate Hotel.

To the south of the village are the ruins of Plas Mawr, an Elizabethan mansion originally owned by the Penry family.

White Mill (Felinwen)

White Mill is a village bypassed by the A40, just east of Abergwili, on the Afon Annell. The watermill, which gives the village its name, still has its 18th/19th century equipment intact but not in use. There is an inn, the White Mill, and mainly older buildings, in all constituting a peaceful refuge from the A40.

Ystradffin (End of the Valley Floor)

Ystradffin is situated just below Llyn Brianne Reservoir, adjacent to the RSPB Dinas Nature Reserve. All that remain today are the church, Ystradffin Farm and a few houses.

The little church is dedicated to St Paulinas, the teacher of St David. By the 9th century the religious community consisted of several buildings. The church was given to the Cistercians of Strata Florida who would have farmed the area and possibly mined for lead. The church was rebuilt in 1821.

Near the church the Environment Agency has a station for gauging the depth of water in the River Towy. The flow of the river is in part controlled by the giant Llyn Brianne Dam, to ensure that sufficient water is available for extraction at Nantgaredig where it is treated and used to provide drinking water across a large area of South Wales. In

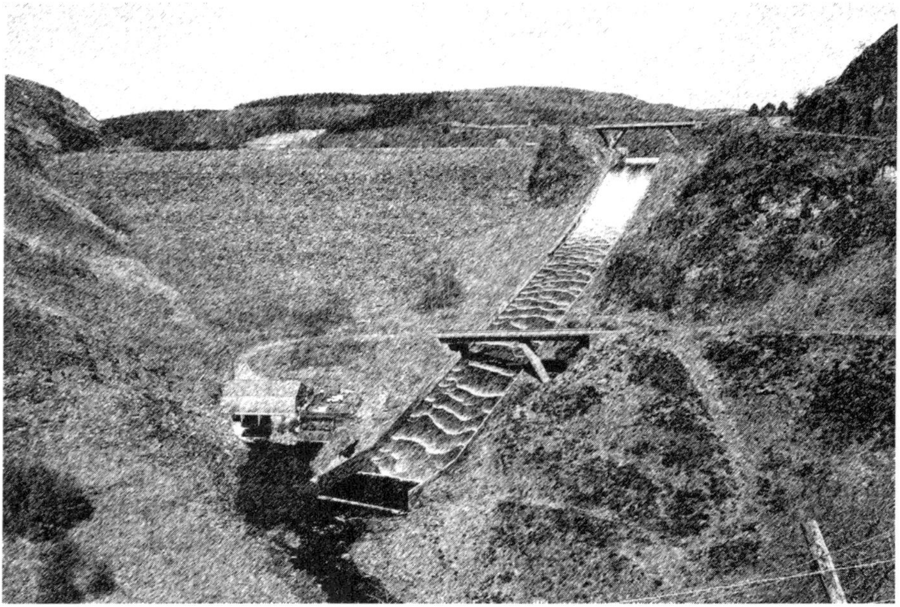

Llyn Brianne Slipway, Ystradffin

1996 the dam was heightened and a hydro electric plant added. The dam is the highest in Britain and reputed to be the largest clay core constructed dam in the world. It offers magnificent views, including the spectacular plumes produced from the turbines, as well as the opportunity for cycling, riding and walking. This area is among the remotest in mid Wales and the forests above the dam are home to red squirrels.

Ystradffin Farmhouse is now a centre for pony trekking, but was once the scene of a fabled romance.

In 1530, Thomas Jones was born out of wedlock to the squire of Porthyffynnon near Tregaron and Catherine, an illegitimate daughter of the Wynn family. Thomas was well educated and possibly because of religious persecution sought refuge in Geneva during the reign of Mary Tudor. He returned to Wales on the accession of Elizabeth I and received a full pardon for all his unspecified crimes and actions. He was a poet and studied heraldry and genealogy, compiling the family trees of the wealthy families of the area. He married Joan Williams, the widow of Ystradffin, albeit in later life and was a magistrate and Sheriff of Carmarthen. He died in 1609. His genealogy tables still form an important source of information on the history of prominent Welsh families and books of his poems are held at the British Library.

Legend, however, has him as Twm Sion Cati, the Welsh Robin Hood with stories of his cunning and hiding from the Sheriff of Carmarthen in a cave in what is now the Dinas Nature Reserve. His exploits were told in the BBC Television series *Hawksmoor*. Stories abound of his exploits. In one story he is carrying a large sum of money and realises that he is to be robbed. He pretends that the money is in his saddlebags and when a highwayman catches him, he throws the bags in a pool and while the highwayman is retrieving the bags Twm steals his horse. In another Twm waylays and robs a rich man and his daughter of cash and jewels but is so smitten by the daughter that he returns the jewellery. He then woos her and after threatening to cut her hand off if she didn't marry him they get married. The only problem with the story is that Thomas and Joan were in their seventies when they tied the knot!

The legends are probably just legends, but the cave in the nature reserve can be visited.

Ystradowen (Owen's Vale)

Ystradowen is a former mining village between Cwmllynfell and Upper Cwmtwrch on the A4068. It occupies a narrow strip of Carmarthenshire between the Afon Twrch and the Afon Llynfell. Apart from the ribbon development along the main road, the village has a more rural feel on Penygraig Road.

There was no mine in the village, though above the village and to the east was Henllys Vale Colliery and lime kiln. The chimney is still standing, just under a mile from the end of Penygraig Road. The colliery had only a short life, opening in 1898 and closing in 1914. The area across the Afon Twrch has seen extensive opencast mining, but has now been restored.

A large natural mound of sand known as Tomen Owen can be seen in Ystradowen just to the north of the main road. It is thought to be the result of retreating glaciers at the end of the last Ice Age.

Glossary

Chapel of Ease

A chapel of ease is a chapel built for the use of worshippers in an area of a parish not within easy distance of the parish church. Chapels attached to large mansions were normally chapels of ease. Normally they were not licensed for burials. In Wales such chapels were sometimes used for services by denominations other than the Established Church. The Anglican Church ceased to be the Established Church in Wales in 1924.

Commote and Hundred

Prior to the Norman Conquest Wales was divided for local government purposes into cantrefs which were further divided into a unit called a cwmwd. A cantref consisted of 100 Trefs or settlements. Half or a third of a cantref was a cwmwd. After the conquest these became hundreds and commotes. Carmarthenshire was divided into eight hundreds.

Turnpikes

The road system in Wales had been neglected over many centuries with a lack of bridges and boulder strewn roads. In an attempt to improve the road network, Turnpike Trusts had been established in the late 18th century and the number of Trusts and toll gates had expanded by the 1830s. While new roads and bridges had been constructed, Trusts were often badly administered and the revenues misused by the trustees. Toll gates proliferated and hit the farmers taking animals to market or collecting lime for fertilizer hard. Tolls could cost more than the value of a load of lime. The Rebecca Riots 1839-43 forced reforms and eventually County Councils took over the maintenance of the roads.

Weeping Chancel

A feature of a number of older churches is what is known as a weeping chancel, where the chancel or altar end is out of line with the nave of the church. This was to represent Christ's head tilted to one side on the cross.

Bibliography

The Antiquities of Langharne and Pendine Mary Curtis, 1871
The Beauties of England and Wales Vol XVIII South Wales Thomas Rees, 1815
The Book of South Wales, The Bristol Channel, Monmouthshire and the Wye Charles Frederick Cliffe, 1848
Carmarthen and its Neighbourhood William Spurrell, 1860
Carmarthenshire Historian
Cambrian Superstitions W Howells, 1831
Dyfed Archaeological Trust
Historical Notes on the Counties of Glamorgan, Carmarthen and Cardigan John Rowland,1806
History of Caio Fred S Jones, 1904
The History of Parliament Online
The Innkeeper's Album W F Deacon, 1823
The Mabinogion Translated by Lady Charlotte Guest
The Place-Names of Wales (Second Edition) Thos. Morgan (Skewen), 1912
A Topographical Dictionary of South Wales Samuel Lewis, 1849
Tours in Wales 1803-1814 Richard Fenton
Wanderings and Excursions in South Wales Thomas Roscoe, 1844
Welsh Biography Online (National Library of Wales)
Wild Wales George Borrow, 1862
www.coflein.gov.uk
Wynford Vaughan-Thomas's Wales

The following websites give more in depth information on the areas they cover than is possible in this book:

www.welshcoalmines.co.uk
www.llanelli-history.co.uk
www.cwmammanhistory.co.uk
www.llandeilo.org